# Peasant
# Fires

Indiana University Press ॐ Bloomington & Indianapolis

The Drummer preaching to the pilgrims at Nik-
lashausen. Woodcut by Michael Wolgemuth or
William Pleydenwurff from Hartmann Schedel,
*Liber chronicarum* (Nuremberg, 1493). *Courtesy
Lilly Library, Indiana University.*

# Peasant Fires

## The Drummer of Niklashausen

Richard Wunderli

The paper used in this publication meets the
minimum requirements of American National
Standard for Information Sciences—Perma-
nence of Paper for Printed Library Materials,
ANSI Z39.48-1984.

∞ ™

Manufactured in the United States of America

Library of Congress Cataloging-in-Publication
Data

Wunderli, Richard M.
    Peasant fires : the drummer of Nik-
lashausen / Richard Wunderli.
        p.  cm.
    Includes bibliographical references (p.    ).
    ISBN 0-253-36725-5 (cloth : alk. paper).
— ISBN 0-253-20751-7
(paper : alk. paper)
    1. Böhm, Hans, ca. 1450–1476. 2. Nik-
lashausen Region (Germany)—Religious life
and customs. 3. Niklashausen Region (Germany)—Social life and customs. 4. Niklashausen Region (Germany)—Politics and
government. 5. Christian pilgrims and pilgrimages—Germany—Niklashausen—History. 6.
Mary, Blessed Virgin, Saint—Cult—
Germany—Niklashausen. I. Title.
BR857.N55W86 1992
943'.471-dc20                        92-6104

1 2 3 4 5 96 95 94 93 92

It's so unfair. People suffered, worked, thought. So much wisdom, so much talent. And they're forgotten as soon as they die. We must do everything possible to keep their memories alive, because we will be treated in the same way ourselves. How we treat the memory of others is how our memory will be treated. We must remember, no matter how hard it is.

—*Testimony: The Memoirs of Dmitri Shostakovich*

# CONTENTS

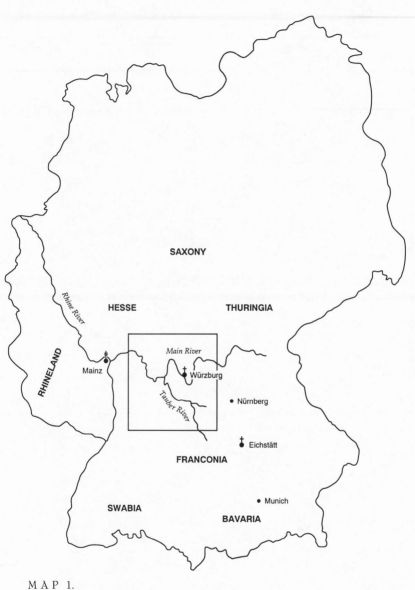

MAP 1.
Germany, with focus on
south-central region.

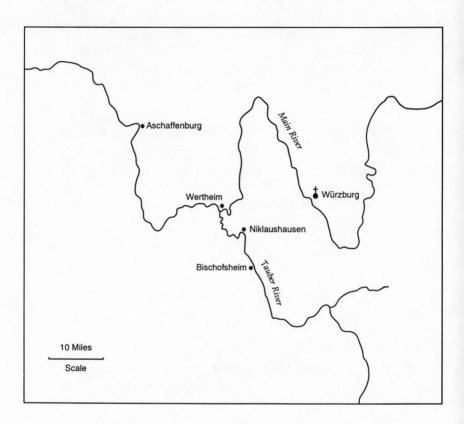

MAP 2.

Tauber and Main River valleys
*(enlargement from Map 1).*

# AUTHOR'S NOTE

I wrote this book for people who are not professional historians in order to introduce them to late medieval Germany, to German scholarship (little of which has been translated into English), and to a (my) process of thinking about history. In almost any bookstore we may find works in English, both popular and scholarly, on fifteenth-century England, France, and Italy— but precious little on Germany. F. R. H. Du Boulay's wonderfully lucid *Germany in the Later Middle Ages* is a welcome exception. Indeed, a cursory glance at book titles about Germany might lead one to believe that German history began in 1933. Germans, more so than the rest of us, daily feel the dead hand of the past on their lives. We must explore that past if we are to make sense of Germany and its people. As professional historians we may know much about German history, but we have done a poor job of conveying it—especially that of medieval Germany—to the reading public. This book is my small contribution to rectify that omission and to help make history again the language of an informed public.

I had the good fortune to have two talented colleagues, Professors Murray Ross and Robert Sackett, critique earlier versions of this book and, hence, help clarify both its style and content. I, of course, take all blame for any of the book's faults.

Although I did not write this book for professional historians, I wish to dedicate it to an extraordinary historian and teacher—my teacher—Professor Robert Brentano of the University of California, Berkeley, as a personal *festschrift*. He, more than anyone else, will understand what I have attempted here.

# Peasant
# Fires

# I

## Enchanted Time

Hans Behem's sheep were settled down for the night. Across the meadow Hans could see the black silhouetted hills of the Tauber Valley against an overcast sky faintly aglow from a full moon. Small, lumpy bundles that were his sheep huddled in groups of eight or ten in brown dirt patches where they had nosed through the snow to find meager shoots of grass. Hans was a young man, perhaps in his early twenties although he probably could not have given his exact age. He was a peasant, a serf, a common herdsman over sheep belonging to other peasants and lords from the village of Niklashausen in the Tauber Valley of south-central Germany.

It was Saturday evening during Lent in 1476. Perhaps early April. The winter had been especially hard and long this year. Deep drifts of snow covered the ground throughout Carnival and Lent, and would continue even through Easter and May Day. Hans, like everybody else, had suffered through the intense, unrelenting cold, and had feared for spring fodder for his animals. He and other peasants faced the coming starvation; the hungry time of Lent might not end unless the weather changed. It seemed as if God had turned his full wrath upon mankind.

During that cold spring night in the common meadows, young Hans huddled under his sheepskin cloak and played on his shepherd's pipe the mournful tunes of the hills of the Tauber Valley. Earlier during the day he had also beat on the little drum that hung about his neck, practicing songs that he performed on the streets of Niklashausen.

From out of the black hills a light appeared, shimmering above the ground, at first faint but then glowing radiantly bright. It gradually formed into the shape and countenance of a young woman, with hands extended, wearing a white gown, and on her head a thin crown wrought with delicately formed crosses. She called to Hans by name as one of her chosen shepherds, and told him to fear not. Hans recognized immediately that she was the Mother of God, the Virgin Mary, to whom he was especially devoted. He had worshipped before her picture many times at her shrine in the little parish church in Niklashausen. He had knelt before the shrine, staring into her serene, wise face, beseeching her as the Queen of Heaven to intercede with God the King and with her Son for mercy. Now she appeared to him, just as he had always seen her, with the same crown, the same extended hands, the same radiantly white dress appropriate for her absolutely pure state of virginity, and the same serene, wise face.

With a gentle voice that softly echoed through the night and over the light bleating of the sheep, the Mother of God spoke to Hans. She told him that both God and her Son were angry with mankind and were chastising all peoples with the dreadful cold and snow. People were consumed by their vanities, she said, and did not worship the Heavenly Family as was their due. Vanities. Evil mankind was obsessed by their vanities, even in this Lenten season of self-sacrifice.

*act as a Jesus*

Henceforth, she said to the young shepherd, Hans was to convey to the world the wishes of God through her, the Mother of God and Queen of Heaven, the Virgin Mary. Hans was ordered to preach to God's people. But first he must strip himself of his own vanities: Hans was ordered to go to the portal of the village church of Niklashausen, the Frauenkirche, the church dedicated to the Virgin, and there publicly he was to burn his drum and his shepherd's pipe. Then he was to preach in Niklashausen, and the Mother of God would instruct him what to say.

The Virgin appeared to Hans many times after that Saturday evening. Just as Hans had made a bonfire of his vanities—his drum and his pipe—so must his listeners discard and burn their vanities, she said, in order to avoid the hammer blows of God's anger: women were to take off their fancy neckerchiefs and their wigs of braided hair; men were to discard their fashionable doublets with slit sleeves and their abominable pointed shoes. All such vanities were to be consumed in the public bonfires of the vanities. God's wrath could be terrible, as the fierce winter had shown. Rebellious mankind must seek voluntary poverty and cry out to God for mercy for their sins. Disobedience could only bring more cold, pestilence, and hunger.

God was angry with mankind, the Mother of God told Hans, and most of all He was angry with the clergy for their sins. "Preach to my faithful people at my shrine at Niklashausen," she instructed, "and tell them that my Son neither is able nor wishes to endure any longer the avarice, pride, and luxury of the clergy and priests. Unless they amend themselves immediately, the entire world will be endangered by their wickedness."

The Virgin often spoke to Hans and instructed him as he preached. His voice in reality was her voice from heaven. She told him to cry out to her faithful people to make a pilgrimage to her shrine at Niklashausen, and there—and only there—would they find full forgiveness of their sins. The Virgin promised that those who lived in luxury with their privileges—the clergy, the nobility, the knights, yea, even the pope and the emperor—would lose their privileges and wealth and live like poor peasants. Nobody would hunger anymore because

*doing sacrifices in order to reap the benefits of god instead of being punished by god*

*emphasizes the social gap*

the forests and the waters of the earth would be held in common. And as for the clergy: for their pride, insolence, and greed, and for their oppression of the poor, they should all be killed. This is what the Virgin, with her gentle voice and wise smile, told Hans to preach: her message was a call to revolution and bloodshed.

I made up most of that. What the records in fact say is that Hans Behem—"the Drummer" as he was contemptuously called—claimed to have had visions or experienced apparitions of the Virgin. Evidence for the cold weather comes from one of Hans' sermons, and the words of the Virgin come from a historical account many years later, in 1514, by Johann Trithemius. Beyond that we know very little except what Hans' enemies—the clergy whom Hans said ought to be killed—chose to tell us. The details of the apparition can only exist in our imaginations: we do not know whether he really thought he saw the Virgin or made it up. And if he did experience something, we do not know where it took place, or when (a casual comment by one of his enemies said it was during Lent), or how many visions he had. We do not know how old Hans was, or what his social position as a shepherd was, or even what kind of animals he herded. What may be gleaned from our sparse records is that the followers of Hans believed he conversed regularly with the Mother of God, and that her message was a call to social revolution.

What follows is Hans' story, from its misty, mysterious beginnings, through the great pilgrimage to Niklashausen that rocked all of southern Germany for a few months in 1476, to its violent conclusion.

The great French medievalist Marc Bloch once said that the "good historian is like the giant of the fairy tale. He knows that wherever he catches the scent of human flesh, there his quarry lies." Bloch meant more than that, of course. He also argued that we should root around anywhere and everywhere for useful information that will help us understand what it means to be human. No barriers, no preconceived notions should stop us. We must comprehend the material world of climate, disease, production, and reproduction, as well as the mental world of myth, religion, fantasy, stories, and dreams. And, like all good historians, Bloch was fascinated by the thought processes of the historian thinking about history. To find the human of the past is to find the historian of the present; they are inseparable.

What I am about to tell is Hans' story, but it is also about how we think about Hans and history, how we make sense of the historical forces that shaped and molded his existence. I have used the story of Hans Behem, the Drummer of Niklashausen, to expose some of the great historical forces, both material and mental, that shaped much of Germany on the eve of the Reformation. The young shepherd boy appears to me as a roughly cut jewel on which a beam of light is concentrated: its irregular facets break up the light to illuminate the surrounding darkness in beautiful and unexpected ways.

Today we have little evidence with which to reconstruct the story of Hans Behem and his pilgrimage to Niklashausen: a few documents and scattered bits of indirect information which were prepared by people with their own peculiar notions of reality. And we have modern historians with their own assumptions about reality who try to make sense of the evidence by using reason, knowledge, and imagination. Historians interpret the documents; historians interpret each other; historians interpret themselves as a factor in other interpretations.

Throughout this book I have quoted extensively from the surviving documents in order to force readers to join with me in making sense of them, that is, to become inquisitive of the documents and of my interpretations.

The process of making sense out of the past is like describing an image as seen through a series of distorted mirrors: each mirror reflects the image into another distorted mirror as each mirror reshapes "reality." Out of the puzzling set of reflections and refractions, we construct an idealized, coherent picture of what happened. To change the metaphor, we construct a narrative or melody line of events, joined with analytical accents or accompaniment to give the narrative depth and texture. The narrative, then, becomes our past reality. We impose coherence on chaos.

Much descriptive background must necessarily precede Hans' story if we are to comprehend what happened in Niklashausen in 1476. Both the melody and the accompaniment of the story make up its thesis: that Hans and his peasant-pilgrims reacted to their changing material conditions (over which they had no control or understanding) by making an appeal to supernatural forces to find justice for their discontent and meaning for their misery; they expressed their discontent, anger, and resentment in their own peculiar language of guilt, longing for salvation (material and spiritual), and a desire for peasant, village justice. That is, they constructed their own narratives of their past—based on powerful Christian social myths—to understand their material present. They were not peculiar in their narrative-myth-history making: in our own time we have experienced two other powerful social myths, National Socialism and Marxist Communism, that have appealed to a past "narrative" to explain the material present.

So, when we hear the wondrous fantasies and angry songs of Hans Behem—the narratives of peasant Christianity—we hear voices of those people, the German peasantry, whose voices had been lost to history, muffled by the incessant hum of literate elite-culture. We must accustom our ears to strangely haunting sounds of peasant dissonance.


What do we know about Hans Behem? Very little. In 1476 he was described as a boy or a "youth"—*der jüngling*. It is difficult to know what this means. Calling him a youth had less to do with his biological age than with his social position. Nevertheless, Hans perhaps was in his late teens or early twenties. We may be quite certain that he was a herder of animals, but what sort of animal is a mystery. The earliest accounts refer sometimes to his "sheep" and other times to his "brute beasts," which may be cows. Later accounts from a generation after

Hans' death—accounts that especially reveal a mean-spirited, mocking hostility to Hans—call him a swineherd or a "pastor of pigs."

Hans spent much of his time alone in the fields and meadows, alone with his fantasies and dreams, composing songs and brooding, we are told, on the unseen spirits that assailed him. Periodically he went to his nearby village of Niklashausen, and perhaps to other villages as well, where he earned a few pennies as a musician, again we are told, playing in taverns. He may have gone as far away as Wertheim or Bischofsheim, about ten miles in either direction from Niklashausen along the Tauber River, or even to Würzburg, about fifteen miles away; and there during Carnival and festivals Hans may have played his drum and pipe for the wild festivities of song and dance.

It was Hans' musical talent that chroniclers and writers singled out; they called him "the Drummer" or, less often, "the Piper." One suspects that calling him the Drummer was the most degrading thing his enemies could think of: not the Peasant, or the Serf, or the Shepherd, or the Boy—but the Drummer. For what could be more foolish during the folk festivals of Carnival than the boy who beat a drum? Perhaps Hans' drumming summed up for his enemies the monotony and simplicity of his message. Boom, boom, boom, he struggled to articulate . . . ba boom. So Hans' enemies also called him (in German) a *spieler*, a player, and his pilgrimage to Niklashausen (in Latin) a *joculus*, a game or the silliness of Carnival; in other words, he was even lower than a peasant because he was a mere player, and merely a child, in society rather than a worker.

Hans the Drummer, chroniclers tell us, banged his drum and sang his songs in the village of Niklashausen. He was a local folk singer. Like any other entertainer, he knew his audience well: the peasants, the poor folk, and the pilgrims who drifted in and out of Niklashausen to go to market or to visit the shrine of the Virgin Mary at the Frauenkirche. Hans had to know their hopes and pain and humor in order to sing their songs and collect his few pennies. He spoke their language.

Hans was born in a region of south-central Germany that we call Franconia, in the small village of Helmstadt, which is not far from

Niklashausen on the Tauber River. Hans belonged to the Tauber Valley, to Niklashausen. Niklashausen still exists as a cluster of houses, nestled at the confluence of the Lauersbach stream and the slow-moving Tauber. The Tauber River flows north past Bischofsheim and Niklashausen and empties into the Main River at Wertheim. During the Middle Ages it carried no important traffic in goods, people, or ideas. There is nothing we know about medieval Niklashausen to distinguish it from any other village—except for Hans' preaching and pilgrimage during a few astonishing months in 1476.

Hans and Niklashausen belonged to three separate jurisdictions. Niklashausen was in the secular jurisdiction of the *Grafschaft* (county) of *Graf* (count) Johann III of Wertheim. It belonged also to the spiritual jurisdiction of the archbishop of Mainz. But Hans as a person, because he was from Helmstadt in the diocese of Würzburg, came under the authority of the bishop of Würzburg. Thus, in my story there will be three authorities (and their many helpers) who will have to confront Hans and deal with his incendiary call for social egalitarianism and the murder of all priests: Count Johann of Wertheim, Archbishop Dieter von Isenberg of Mainz, and Bishop Rudolph von Sherenberg of Würzburg.

Hans Behem lived in an enchanted world. So did his contemporaries, including his enemies among the clergy who were university educated. The natural world for them was bounded by a mere translucent, porous barrier that led to the more powerful realm of spirits, devils, angels, and saints. The "other" realm was "real." It was in the "other" realm that the inexplicable became explicable: here, weather was formed, pestilences decreed or abated, the fertility of crops and animals and humans decided upon. The temporal, workaday world was a sort of illusion, beyond which was the reality of the spiritual world.

At certain periods during the year or at certain places, people could come especially close to that sacred other-realm. These were the feast days, or holy days, that were dedicated to specific saints or to Christ. These were sacred times. So, for Hans and his contemporaries, time

8

did not run relentlessly forward, as it does for us who are bound by clocks, so much as it pulsated like shafts of heavenly light. Periodically the shafts of time-light flooded the earth or were concentrated on a specific place. Then time came to a standstill. Medieval people measured the year in pulsations of timeless states. Sometimes the pulses appeared only in a local parish church during the celebration of a particular saint, sometimes they lasted only a day, sometimes several days. For Hans Behem in Niklashausen in 1476, sacred time lasted for almost three months.

Time between the pulses existed as a mere interlude, as either a memory of the last sacred time or an anticipation of the next one. It was during the first half of the calendar year, from Advent to Midsummer's Day, that is, from December to late June, that the pulsations of radiant timelessness were strongest and most frequent. Below are some of the major festivals which organized the sacred half of 1476—and which organize this book:

Advent (December 3, 1475–December 24, 1475)
Twelve Days of Christmas, from Christmas to Epiphany (December 25, 1475–January 6, 1476)
Carnival, to Shrove Tuesday (January–February 26, 1476)
Lent, from Ash Wednesday to Easter Eve (February 27–April 13, 1476)
Easter Day (April 14, 1476)
Easter week to Pentecost (April 14–June 2, 1476)
*Walpurgisnacht* (April 30, 1476)
Corpus Christi (June 13, 1476)
Nativity of John the Baptist, Midsummer's Day (June 24, 1476)

Mingled among the major festivals throughout the calendar year were many saint's days. Some were major holidays, some minor and local, but all brought heaven and earth closer together: the workaday world briefly came to resemble—if only by analogy and often through irony—the enchanted realm.

The enchanted realm was that half of the year when the heavens opened and human time became heavenly time. During those months in 1476, Hans Behem experienced his visions, preached his sermons, and attracted tens of thousands of peasant-pilgrims to the tiny village of Niklashausen. The pilgrims were called not just by Hans Behem, the shepherd boy, but also by the Virgin Mary. It was a voice from the other, enchanted realm that drew them irresistibly to Niklashausen. It was the voice of the most powerful saint of the Middle Ages.

Indeed, the Virgin was more than a saint. She occupied a position in heaven only slightly lower than the Godhood itself. During the Middle Ages her hold on popular imagination intensified, and popular passion burned for her ever brighter until she dominated fifteenth-century religious sensibilities. Sermons from every pulpit in Europe recounted pious tales, called *exempla,* of the good things that happen to those who venerate the Virgin. Such *exempla* were preserved in books and then carried to pulpits throughout Europe, usually by Franciscan or Dominican friars, who were especially devoted to the Virgin and who were the primary propagators of her cult. One example:

> One day a friar was standing intently at prayer when he saw the heavens open up in a vision: and there he saw the Queen of Mercy before her Son, with hands extended, humbly on her knees; for she had knelt down submissively praying for a certain sinner known throughout the land for his evil ways. Briefly stated, the man was possessed by the devil so that he neither feared God nor cared for his fellow humans. The aforementioned friar saw this but did not understand what the outcome of the Virgin's prayers was, because the vision suddenly disappeared. Therefore, the friar, wishing to know the conclusion of the matter, decided to visit the evil man to discover whether the power of the Virgin was able to obtain grace for him. He went to the man's home, fearing that the man would be hostile to him. But the man greeted the friar, received him honorably, and said:

"Brother, I have thus far lived badly and have offended God in all ways most grievously: I ask you to help me so that I may please God and save my soul. I am prepared to do anything." Having said this, the man humbly and devoutly confessed his sins to the friar and completely changed his life. Thereafter he lived an exemplary life that amazed all who knew him. Behold, even in this case, the Queen of Mercy deems worthy to demonstrate her benevolence by obtaining grace for anybody to be saved: one need only ask for her help, with hands extended, humbly on one's knees; and she will carry this supplication to her dear Child, her Son, before Whom she humbly and sweetly kneels.

For an instant we are allowed a glimpse into the enchanted realm. The actions of the Virgin had immediate impact on earth. Her time was God's time: her space was God's space. Heaven and earth were a time-space continuum. And the *exemplum* suggests a peculiar point of view that was repeated in many other *exempla:* the Virgin's mercy transcends human justice and human laws; what matters is not innocence or guilt, only the veneration due her.

The Virgin Mary had a special regard for shepherds, such as Hans Behem, and for the dumb animals of the fields, because shepherds and beasts were the first to honor her and Jesus at the Nativity. At least this was what the gospel of Luke taught—in contrast to that of Matthew, who spoke only of three Magi from the East. Luke's version became the controlling document, a sort of charter myth, for much of the legendary material in writing and art that accrued around the historical Mary. Actually, Luke did not mention animals at all at the Nativity. They were a later addition that was absorbed into the Mary story from old, pre-Christian, Mediterranean motifs that associated "mother" and "fertility" with tame animals in the field. And the "manger" of Jesus' birth more correctly was a "crib," and it probably was in a tent rather than in a stable. But in the early church there already was fashioned a Nativity scene in which the first witnesses to the birth of Christ were oxen, asses, sheep, and shepherds.

11

By the eleventh century, the cult of the Virgin Mary had burst upon European consciousness. The radiance of her cult emanated over Europe, often blocking out the presence of other invisible saints. Although popular belief elevated her in stature to be the "Queen of Heaven" and sinless (alone with her Son) in her Immaculate Conception, Mary never forsook her special protection of shepherds and dumb animals.

Throughout medieval Europe, miraculous discoveries of buried, small statues of Mary were made by shepherds on their lonely grazing lands. Images were found often enough for modern scholars to classify them as a miracle type called the shepherd's cycle. The statues themselves then became the object of veneration at a shrine dedicated to the Virgin, a place bathed in a beam of light from heaven where worshippers could approach the Holy. The statues possessed miraculous powers from heaven, directly from the enchanted realm, from the Virgin herself, powers that cured illnesses in body and soul.

But Hans, unlike other shepherds, did not find an image of the Virgin. He saw her bodily in an apparition. This too was not unusual, because Mary, more than other saints, could appear whole to humans; at her death—if indeed, as some questioned, she died at all—she was taken bodily and directly to heaven. This was her Assumption: Jesus cradled her soul in His arms and the apostles carried her body to heaven. In any case, it is the version of the Golden Legend (or story of her life) that had become commonplace in medieval Europe. Because Mary was taken bodily directly to heaven, there were no bone relics of Mary on earth as there were in copious quantities of other saints. Churches had locks of her hair, cloaks, belts, and vials of breast milk, but no bones. If Mary could not sin, then she could not suffer the pains of sins, which are death and the putrefaction of the flesh. Thus Mary, with body intact, already resurrected, was able to appear whole in a visit from the enchanted realm to humans. She appeared to Hans in a field and spoke to him. She had selected one of her favored shepherds to convey God's displeasure with sinful humanity.

The Mother of God was the only really appropriate mediator between God and man. Her position in heaven was special. She was at once mother, queen, and bride to the Godhead: she was the Mother of God, the Queen of Heaven—and nobody in medieval Europe doubted the hidden influence of queens on kings—and the Bride of Christ, bound in pure Platonic love to her Son and Husband. Actually, she was only an unofficial, but widely accepted, Queen of Heaven; only recently, in 1954, did Pope Pius XII officially crown her Queen. As Queen, so preachers told their audiences, Mary represents the destiny of all good Christians, to be united bodily with God; as Bride, they said, she is love yet the denial of earthly, contaminated desire. As Mother, Bride, and Queen, Mary wielded extraordinary influence over the two males in her household, the stern but just Father and the forgiving Son. No other saint in the extended spiritual family of heaven could match her influence.

Other saints, such as George and Nicholas and Anne and Catherine and a multitude of others, spoke for a specific location or particular group of people: George for England, Nicholas for merchants and students, Anne for miners, Catherine for young girls. No Christian was without a protective saint.

Mary was different. She transcended borders and social rankings—with the exception of her favorites at the bottom of society, shepherds. But only a saint with the boundless love of Mary could care for shepherds. Not surprisingly, more churches in Europe were dedicated to Mary than to any other saint. Even in Niklashausen, a town calling on the powerful St. Nicholas, the lone parish church was dedicated to the Virgin Mary, *die Frauenkirche*. It had a small Marian shrine that drew occasional pilgrims—until 1476.

So pervasive was the Virgin Mary in medieval, fifteenth-century German sensibility that she meets us at every turn, in words and images, in all forms of expression. Mary, in allegory, was often seen as a rose, and consequently dominates the rosary—or garland of roses, *der Rosenkrantz*—which came into widespread popular use during the fifteenth century. Franciscan friars especially popularized the prayer beads as a way of shaping popular piety through memorized prayers. And the most recited prayer on the rosary was the *Ave Maria,* which reached its final form during the late fifteenth and early sixteenth centuries. It was the most often recited prayer in late medieval Christianity. Laymen joined together in brotherhoods during the fifteenth century to recite the rosary. In the cathedral of Cologne there were 5,000 members of a "rosary brotherhood," and a contemporary Dominican friar calculated that each week (in 1475), 700,000 *Ave Marias* were said from that brotherhood alone. To Mary, in the enchanted realm, the din of invocations from the world below must have sounded as indistinct as great waves against a shore.

But the Virgin heard the voice of a simple German shepherd, and appeared to him.

We must begin the story, before Hans' vision, with his joyful world of music and dance during Carnival. This takes us into enchanted time and space where social structure dissolved. After midsummer of 1476, we will emerge again into normal time of structure, power, and authority.

The story of Hans Behem is a tragedy in the medieval sense of the word: it begins happy and ends sad. So we begin with Carnival. Perhaps the Drummer played his pipe and drum then, and perhaps he really danced on a big drum as Bishop Rudolph of Würzburg claimed.

# II
# Carnival

There is an old story that was told and retold throughout Europe about a helpless boy who is mistreated by his stepmother and those in authority, and how he exacts revenge. It appears in many versions, often in song. In the following tale from a fifteenth-century English source, those who make life hell for the boy are his stepmother and her lover-friend, Friar Tobias. The boy is called Jack, but in my version I will use the German equivalent, Hans, or better, the diminutive Hänsel. With wild, carnivalesque humor, Hänsel finds justice against his tormentors. But he must resort to magic, that is, he must appeal for help from the other, enchanted realm for his special powers.

The story begins with a dispute between the father and the stepmother over what to do about Hänsel. The stepmother wants to send him away to fend for himself in the world, but the father decides to allow the boy to stay for another year and work in the fields as a cowherd.

So, the next day, Hänsel went into the fields. Presently, he came to a meadow and sat down in the grass to enjoy his dinner, but the food his stepmother gave him was so bad that he couldn't eat it. As the boy sat alone, an old man came to him, gave a greeting, and told Hänsel how hungry he was. Could the boy spare some food? Hänsel replied, "God save me, but you are right welcome to such poor victuals as I have." The old man ate the food and was happy.

"Son," the old man said, "you have given me food, and so I will give you three things, whatever you want." Hänsel was very excited and his first choice was a bow and arrows so that he could shoot birds for food. The old man gave him a bow and arrows and said that no matter how many times he shot, he would always hit the mark. Hänsel laughed for joy, and for his second wish he asked for a pipe to play on: "If I had a pipe, no matter how large or small, then I would be content with all my wishes, for then I could play music out here in the fields." The old man gave Hänsel a beautiful pipe and promised him that "whatever living creature hears it shall have no power to resist, but will laugh and leap about."

"Now," said the old man, "what is your third choice?" But the boy said that he had enough for his poor trade as a cowherd. The old man insisted on a third choice, so Hänsel said, "At home I have a cruel stepmother who is full of pride and torments me. She looks at me with hatred in her eyes. And so I wish that when she looks angrily at me so, she will let loose a mighty fart that will ring throughout the house." The old man agreed: "Whenever she looks you in the face in anger, her tail shall give wind to the horn so loudly that whoever hears it will laugh at her and bring her to shame." Then the old man departed.

That night, as Hänsel drove his cows home from the fields, he blew his pipe. And the cows, walking in a row, began to dance; and so the skipping, happily mooing beasts followed Hänsel into his father's farmyard.

The boy then went to his father's hall, where he and the stepdame were at supper. Hänsel asked for some food, for he had not eaten all day. The father threw the boy a chicken wing. But this made the stepmother furious that he should get anything, and she stared at him with hatred in her eyes. And with that she let loose with such a blast from her tail that others throughout the house were all aghast. Everyone roared with laughter at the woman, who grew red with shame and wished she were invisible.

"By God," said Hänsel, "that gun was fully charged and shot, and could have cracked a stone."

At this remark, the stepmother cast him a nasty glance . . . and then let loose another fart that sounded like thunder.

"Did you ever see a woman let her pellets fly more thickly and easily?" said the boy. "Woman, control your telltale bum, for shame!"

"Dame," said the father, "you had better leave the table, for your gear seems not to be in working order."

The stepmother left in burning shame.

Shortly thereafter, a certain Friar Tobias came to the house, and stayed the night—for the stepmother did love this Friar as a saint. When they were alone, she complained to him of Hänsel's cheeky behavior: "He is a wicked boy, a witch; I dare not look upon his face for reasons that are too shameful to tell. For my sake, meet this boy tomorrow and give him a good beating. Make him blind or lame." The friar swore he would beat the boy; and then he took his pleasure of the stepmother.

Early the next morning, Hänsel drove his cows out to the field. He was followed by Friar Tobias, who demanded that the boy explain his evil conduct to his stepmother or he would beat him soundly.

But the boy shrewdly changed the subject: "Why chide me? Come, watch me shoot my arrow. I can hit that small bird way over there in the eye. I'll give him to you." Well, the friar had to see this, and told him to shoot. Hänsel hit the bird right in the eye and it fell down dead in some sharp brier bushes. Friar Tobias ran to the bushes and picked up the bird in astonishment. Meanwhile Hänsel took out his pipe and began to play. The friar could not help but skip around and dance and laugh. As he whirled about among the thorns, the sharp briers tore at his face and clothes, his cape and linen shirt, and even did prick his privy member so that he was bleeding all over.

Hänsel roared with laughter and Friar Tobias begged for mercy and promised never to do him harm. The boy stopped piping and the friar crawled out of the briers, bleeding and in rags. He looked like a madman.

Friar Tobias went to the stepmother and told her of his mishap: "Dame, I came from your son; he and the devil have ruined me and no man may conquer him." At that moment the father came in and the woman shrieked at him that his son had almost killed the holy friar by making him dance among the thorns.

That night, when Hänsel returned home, his father asked what he had done to the friar. The boy replied that he had merely played a mirthful tune on his pipe. "Well then, son, let us hear you play," said the father.

"No, no," cried Friar Tobias, "don't let him play it. By God's love, if he plays that pipe, bind me fast to a post." And so the friar was bound to a post in the middle of the hall, amid many mocking comments.

"Pipe on, Hänsel," said the father.

With that, Hänsel began to play, and every living creature laughed and skipped and leaped about, kicking their legs, now in, now out, and trying to prance about in the air. Everybody danced wildly, including the stepmother. And every time she looked at the boy she let loose a loud, cracking fart. All the friar could do was squirm under the ropes until they cut him, and knock his head against the post. This was his dance.

Hänsel nimbly ran into the street and everybody chased after him, tumbling over each other. The neighbors heard the pipe and came dancing out of their doors and windows. Sick folk in bed and those who were undressed—stark naked—joined in the rough revelry in the street. And Hänsel piped on. Even the lame joined in; and trying to leap about like the others, they tumbled down and had to dance on their hands and knees.

At last a tired Hänsel stopped playing.

The father thought this the best fun that he had had in many a year. But Friar Tobias was enraged and ordered Hänsel to appear before the church court on the following Friday as a suspected witch.

So, on Friday many people flocked to the court for all sorts of cases. At last it was Friar Tobias' turn. He announced loudly to the court that young Hänsel was a witch and should be severely punished. Then the stepmother looked at the boy and called him a devil. At that a mighty fart came out of her tail—and everybody roared with laughter. The gentle judge asked her to tell the court what she knew. But for shame she refused to speak. Friar Tobias then jumped forward and told the judge about the miraculous pipe.

Now, the judge had to hear the pipe for himself, so he told Hänsel to play. As he blew into his pipe everybody leaped up and began to dance: court officials, priests, pimps and prostitutes who were being charged, everybody screamed with laughter and let their arms and legs flail about. Even the judge hopped upon his table and then jumped to the floor with his robe flying. Friar Tobias leaped about as hard as the rest and crashed face to face into the judge. The scribe swung his inkpot, cracking people on the head. Lawyers flung their bills about and bounced off each other.

And the stepmother's bum gave many a fart, *pppfffffttt,* perfuming all the mirth.

Finally the judge cried out, "For God's grace and the love of Mary Mild, pipe no more, boy." But Hänsel said he would stop only if the judge promised to set him free and do him no harm and not allow his stepmother or Friar Tobias to do him wrong. The judge immediately promised to protect him from all his foes.

Hänsel stopped piping. All stood still, exhausted, some laughing with tears in their eyes, some raging as if they were mad.

And so the boy was protected from his evil stepmother and the wicked friar.

Hänsel, the boy cowherd, found justice, but only in fantasy through an appeal to the miraculous enchanted world of magic flutes. For only in the enchanted realm could the powerless reverse roles and find revenge against their tormentors; only then could they control their own lives which otherwise were at the mercy of others. A simple shepherd, in the story above as well as in Niklashausen in 1476, was momentarily empowered to dictate social justice.

In fact, the story of Hänsel, like the real life of Hans Behem in Niklashausen, betrays the utter helplessness of the oppressed to imagine a different social order in the here-and-now. They had to resort to dreams and fantasies, to wild dancing and uncontrollable laughter, for justice and social harmony.

The world of fantasy justice in late medieval Europe was re-enacted ritually several times per year during festival time.

The Drummer. The Piper. *Der Pawker. Der Pfeifer.* Medieval Europe knew many musical instruments, but the lowliest instrument was the drum, closely followed by the shepherd's pipe. Anybody could play a drum, which was a despised instrument in polite society. It was usually associated with mimes and minstrels who performed racy songs in taverns. Hans' enemies indeed claimed that he had performed in taverns—that is, until he had his vision.

But to call Hans a drummer or a piper is also to say that he almost certainly played his drum and pipe at folk festivals. The greatest folk festival was Carnival, that exuberant, enchanted time when common folk ritually acted out fantasy justice. But they acted out their fantasies in bellowing laughter and masquerade, amid games, gambling, ass pinching, displays of huge phallic sausages, and dirty songs. What made Carnival so uninhibited and joyful was that it immediately preceded Lent and was, therefore, just the opposite of everything Lent stood for. If Lent was a grim time of self-sacrifice, abstinence, penance, and soul cleansing, Carnival was a time of indulgence, music, dancing, and roaring, reverberating, uncontrollable laughter.

So Carnival to a greater or lesser degree accompanied the great religious feasts of Epiphany and Lent. It was bound to them in the same way that peasant life was bound to official elite culture: Carnival was part of official culture, yet was a uniquely folk expression in opposition to official culture. Thus, when Hans' enemies among the educated elites referred to him contemptuously as the Drummer, they were referring, I think, to his role in the world of Carnival, to that folk world that glorified fools with so much jeering and foolishness—and that contained, just below the surface, hostility to the ruling order and their solemn feast days.

The great festivals or feasts of the year had been established by the official church, but many of them obviously arose from earlier pagan or folk festivals now lost in the dark forests of custom of the early Middle Ages. Festivals especially show the interdependence of popular (folk) culture and official (elite) culture. By the late Middle Ages, that is, by the fifteenth century in Germany, every festival of the year still bore marks of that symbiosis of the two cultures: every festival had two parts to it, folk and elite, but the two celebrations often seemed to be in opposition. So, following the solemn church ceremony that was celebrated by an official feastday sermon or mass, the folk activities began. Stalls and booths were set up for buying and selling. In short, the solemn day became a market day. Now was the time for copious drinking, eating, and laughter, unlike anything in everyday life and in opposition to the solemn church ceremonies. And even the most solemn church masses at Christmas and Easter were subject to crude, scatological satire, as was the most holy of Christian books, the Bible.

*Inter faeces et urinam nascimur.* "We are born in the midst of urine and feces." So the German historian Will-Erich Peuckert placed at the masthead of his wonderful book on the apocalyptic fifteenth century and Martin Luther. Peuckert published his book in 1948 after working on it throughout the nightmare years of National Socialism, and his slogan touches many levels of irony. For the fifteenth century, it points to Peuckert's bleak vision of the desperate lives of German peasants, but it also certainly refers to the focus of Carnival on the genitals, stomach, and intestines—in short, on the most worldly and least sacred of human actions: defecation.

At the Christmas festival in German cathedral towns, a boy was elected bishop for a day and performed a mock mass: he wore his clothes backward or even dressed as a woman, held the Holy Book upside down, and made bawdy references to genitals from the Book. Where the congregation should be blessed, they were cursed: may the devil fart and give birth to your children; may God piss on your neighbor's fields and give him abundance; may the devil's turd stick in your teeth. Everything was exaggerated and crude: huge bellies, huge genitals, huge belches, huge farts. Everything that was grotesque was a celebration of the material world and mocked the solemnity of the spiritual world of the clergy. And so it went, with parades, processions, mock sermons, mock masses, dirty songs, insults, costumes, masks, drinking, farting, defecating, sexual innuendo—and amateur musicians like Hans Behem playing their drums, whose rhythms everybody knew were suggestive of sexual intercourse.

Often at the center of the festivities was a braying ass: a metaphor for foolish mankind. There was the Feast of the Ass that accompanied the real Feast of the Flight into Egypt, that is, Mary's flight on a donkey with the infant Jesus, which was celebrated during the first week of January. The Feast of the Ass also contained a mock mass, performed by a donkey in clerical robes. He brayed the words of the mass at an altar which had been perfumed with a censor of dung. This was followed by a procession or parade of young clerics, riding in a wagon, throwing animal dung at onlookers as a benediction. During Carnival there also was the mock solemn reading of the Ass's Will. A dying ass hee-haws at the crowd and in donkey talk bequeathes parts of his body to specific people and groups: the ass's head goes to the pope, his ears (and the common symbol of fools) to the cardinals, his voice to the church choir, and so on, until he bequeathes his shit to the peasants.

Medieval people lived in anticipation of a coming festival or in remembrance of one just past. In between festivals was work. There was a rhythm to their lives of work and play, work and play. But it was an uneven rhythm, with the greatest periods of play or celebration clustered in the winter and spring, the heart of Carnival season. As the date of Easter shifted yearly in response to the changing date of the full moon after the vernal equinox, so did other feast days which, like Carnival, were caught in the net of Easter also shift yearly, now pulled forward, now backward, with each springtime full moon. Thus, time followed a routine, but it was fluid time that shifted yearly during the late winter and early spring. Time was not so much a measure of hours and days as it was of ritualized joy, laughter, deprivation, and seriousness.

What Hans Behem saw when he was growing up were the yearly festival rituals and games that were similar in form all over Germany (or, indeed, Europe). Details of celebrations may have differed locally, but the dates of the festivals and their basic structures were largely the same throughout Europe. At festival, the fool reigns, with his donkey's ears, cockscomb, and bells. And out of the laughing, jeering mouth of the fool comes wisdom and common sense that mocks the foolishness of the workaday world. The mock ceremonies of the mass or the rule of the boy bishop or the foolish Lòrd of Misrule—all made fun of the most terrifying exercises of official power. Laughter. Wild, mocking, hooting, guffawing, finger-pointing laughter eased the fears of the powerless who had to face solemn and powerful people during normal, everyday time. In Carnival they had their chance to reduce powerful, privileged people to their own lowly level—defecators all. Their weapon was humor that was also fantasy. Wherever there was authority—and, therefore, solemnity and pomposity—there was Carnival laughter. Even hell in popular, festival representations was by the late fifteenth century increasingly conceived in folk imagination as populated by popes, kings, and other temporal and spiritual authorities. Folk fantasy condemned powerful authorities to hell, just as in their sermons preachers regularly condemned the powerless to hell. During this brief pulsation of timeless time, those who suffered found their liberty, their voice, and their fantasy revenge.

Hans no doubt experienced the crudity and roughness of folk humor, which was aimed at everybody and everything. Nobody was spared. There were mock thrashings of all sorts of people. So, at certain festivals a play-king was elected. He was a fool wearing donkey's ears and bells who "mis-ruled" everything, only to be uncrowned and mock-thrashed. So were real slanderers beaten and forced to run a gauntlet. Real cuckolds and scolding wives and wife-beating husbands were forced to ride an ass with their faces turned to the tail, all accompanied by the din of their neighbors beating pots and pans. In remote German villages, a "stranger" was held captive in a ring of peasants who fiercely whetted their scythes while chanting threatening, bloodcurdling rhymes. Or a "stranger" was forced onto the threshing floor and taught to do the "flail dance." Folk humor could be cruel, but it always contained powerful undercurrents of folk justice, whether to enforce morality such as marital fidelity or to increase folk solidarity against outsiders, or to critique the social order.

The actual festivities of Carnival could last the few days before Lent (in small villages) or several weeks (in large cities). People then entered a "pulsation of time" when time stopped. Modern anthropologists refer to this as "liminal" time, that is, when "normal," forward-moving time stops and people cross over the boundary or passageway (in Latin, the *limes*) into a timeless state, to emerge later renewed. Here, at the threshold of the liminal state, people throughout medieval Europe dressed in masquerade. They became what they were not. The real, grim, everyday world was replaced by its opposite. The common theme of Carnival time was the world turned upside down, inside out. For this was what happened to time itself; it had become its opposite, it had stopped. So it was with people. They became something other than what they were. In some cases the inside-out symbolism was obvious: some people wore their clothes backward and rode their animals facing the tail. But laymen also dressed as clerics or donkeys or bears or dukes or kings or popes, and acted out their new identities in public with mocking solemnity. All expectations of the natural world were reversed. People brayed like asses, and asses talked like men—and the similarity between asses and men became hilariously apparent.

So, folk festivals such as Carnival were occasions of brief, ritualized liberation of common people from the hierarchy of powerful people who normally dominated them in their grim daily lives. For brief, carefully specified periods, common folk were allowed into an enchanted world of freedom, equality, and abundance. The pulsations of liminal time were marked by satire, parody, and laughter at everything that was sacred. By mocking the sacred, people came closer to it through their intimate familiarity with sacred objects and sacred rituals. Therefore, when they returned to normal time, they again held sacred objects in awe. During festival, all people were brought down to the same level: popes, emperors, kings, bishops, all were reduced to their essential bodily functions—eating and defecating. All, in the end, were hardly different from asses. During festival, the material needs of the body reigned supreme. Eat, drink, shit. Free yourself at last from the drab fare of everyday hunger and misery.

Carnival came to an end during the night of Shrove Tuesday (which in 1476 fell on February 26) with great peasant bonfires lit in villages all over Germany. Priests blessed the fires, thus transforming them into a spiritual reality, into something sacred. Young people went from house to house collecting straw and brushwood for the fire. When the great fire was lit, peasants carefully watched the direction of the smoke, for if it blew over the arable fields, then this was a sign that the harvest would be good. And young men dragged a great wooden wheel to the top of their local hill, daubed it with pitch, set in on fire, and then rolled the blazing wheel down the hill; wherever it might roll would be kept safe from hail and violent storms. Often a straw man was constructed and called Death; he was accused of all sorts of thefts of life, then led around the village and burned. Peasants danced around the execution fires of the death of Death, and young men and women leaped over the dying embers of the great bonfire—to ensure fertility, we are told. Peasant fires had great regenerative powers.

For everybody, rich and poor, noble and common, Carnival was a time of gaiety, but it was also a tense time, because the powerless briefly were empowered in enchanted time. How far would common people go when they acted out their role reversals? When Carnival ended and the dying embers of the peasant fires finally flickered out, would the festivities stop and everything return to sober normality? Folk festivals presumably were tolerated by the powerful because the festivities tended to canalize protest against the hierarchy into bounded, ritualized time: in today's imagery of the steam engine we interpret such festivities as a "safety-valve" for letting off steam, or anger. Festivals also periodically reinforced hierarchical authority in the minds of commoners by reminding them how important lords were for keeping real order in real time. For out of the periodical foolishness of liminal time, everything must return to order, which was preferable to the "mis-rule" of role reversal.

But what if there were bad harvests, unusually bad weather, excessively heavy taxation, and widespread hunger and misery around the time of the great winter, spring, and early summer festivals? What then of the language of mockery of authority, of those with abundant food, of those who live off the labor of the poor? The festivities may stop, but the language and imagery of Carnival may continue into normal time and explode into the language of revolt. An illiterate shepherd boy who played a drum in Carnival processions, and who perhaps acted as a religious leader in a reversal of roles, might continue in his play role after Carnival. The call to have the world turned upside down and inside out, to level all ranks, and to abolish all privilege, need not cease after the final bonfire. Timeless time need not be time bound. The bonfires need not burn out.

During Carnival in February 1476, winter snows had been unusually heavy, and the cold biting. Much of southern Germany had suffered crop failure during the previous year. Bavaria and Swabia faced severe famine. To the north of Niklashausen, in the great duchy of Saxony, there had been crop failures also in 1474 and 1475; large numbers of the poor, especially the young, had left their homes without permission to go on a pilgrimage to Wilsnack to beg for bread. Yet, landlords and authorities still collected their rents, tithes, duties, and tolls from peasants. Nobles and the clergy were largely exempt from such exactions. Carnival humor in 1476 must have been bitter and biting.

# III
## Lent

The Virgin Mary, Mother of the Holy Church, charges us today at the beginning of Lent to recall how our captain, Jesus Christ, fought against the Enemy of the human race and how he conquered the three great evils. He is our Teacher and Instructor and we give Him our complete trust that today we also will begin to fight against—and conquer—our three great enemies: our own flesh and blood, the world, and the Evil Spirit. Whichever of you good Christians will conquer these three enemies, you must observe the teachings of our Captain.

So began the series of Lenten sermons by Ulrich Kraft in the late fifteenth century. Lent was just the opposite of Carnival. No more feasting, no more pleasures of the flesh, no more wallowing in the joys of the world. Now was the time to fast. Christians all over Europe were told to conquer the three great enemies, "our own flesh and blood, the world, and the Evil Spirit." The obese, flesh-eating, sausage-wielding voluptuary of the Carnival dramas was now replaced by the emaciated old hag with a fish about her neck. Forty grim, soul-cleansing weekdays and six Sundays awaited believers until the joyful arrival of Easter.

Now was also the time for serious talk. Preachers throughout Germany had many published collections of sermons to draw from for any Sunday or feast day of the year. But one collection was especially used, the *Quadragesimale,* or sermons for Lent (in Latin, Lent is *Quadragesima,* or "forty"). In Germany during the fifteenth century preachers customarily delivered a sermon every day during Lent. All the great preachers of Germany—mostly Dominican and Franciscan friars such as Johann Gritsch, Johann of Werden, and Johann Herolt, or university professors such as Ulrich Kraft—published collections of Lenten sermons for the use of preachers everywhere, calling on the faithful to renounce the flesh and to turn their backs on the world. *Quadragesimale* collections proliferated in Germany more than elsewhere in Europe. The message of Lent was to seek poverty of temporal material goods in order to gain eternal spiritual salvation.

For many people in medieval Europe, particularly peasants, poverty was the normal condition of their everyday existence. Lent only justified and sanctified their misery. The great pilgrimage to Niklashausen was preached by a peasant shepherd, Hans Behem, for a peasant audience with the same Lenten message of "sacred poverty" that friars had preached for centuries. We now turn to peasants, friars, and preachers, who all dignified and enshrined poverty: here we find the powerful social myths that drove peasant-pilgrims from all over Germany to Niklashausen.

Peasants the world over live and have always lived a precarious existence. Anthropologists with some justification have lumped them into a single sociological type and have enclosed their misery under the rubric "the culture of poverty." Indeed, Eric Wolf tells us, they are "peasants" because others with privilege and power in society have trapped them economically into an existence of work and poverty. In turn, peasants enclose themselves in mental prisons of limited expectations and devastating fatalism. There are variations to peasant life, of course, in time and place, but the precariousness of peasant life seems to remain a constant. At best, economic victories of peasants, such as a good harvest, bring small gains. Economic defeats may be fatal. Richard Tawney's bleak imagery of Chinese peasants perhaps can stand for all peasants: they stand in water up to their necks, and the slightest ripple drowns them.

It is the ability of more powerful people such as landlords and political lords to "make ripples" that defines what a peasant is. For peasants belong to "civilization," with its division of labor, its ruling political elite from which peasants are excluded, and its powerful market forces that push and pull peasants as in a magnetic field. Lords have claims on the land, labor, and production of peasants, claims that ultimately are enforced by military arms.

A fifteenth-century German peasant was not allowed to wear a sword; his only possible arms were the hand tools of his trade, the scythe, the flail, the hammer. He was also recognizable by restrictions on his dress, which had been legislated since the time of Charlemagne, and by his lack of privilege—that is, in the medieval sense of privilege as a "private law" that protects a specific group of people. Men and women above peasants had "privileges," whether dress, or right to bear arms, or freedom from taxes; peasants did not.

Hans Behem was a peasant, as were the tens of thousands of men, women, and children who flocked to Niklashausen in 1476 to hear him preach. He was a herder of animals and did not work in the fields. But peasants could be shepherds, millers, brewers, smiths, and stonemasons as well as field workers. What mattered was the legal claim made by the ruling elite on their labor and on whatever they produced.

What I am describing, of course, are general conditions of "peasants," especially late fifteenth-century German peasants. Because the peasant gathering in Niklashausen in 1476 was a "general" movement that swept up peasants from all over central and south

Germany, the general condition of the late fifteenth-century peasantry must concern us. Their material conditions, I think, gave them a peculiar worldview that led them to see their salvation in the visionary shepherd Hans Behem.

What were the material needs of the German peasantry? A peasant household had first to provide whatever was necessary to live, and then enough surpluses for next year's crops and for the replacement and repair of equipment. This was the bare minimum for sustained survival. But a German peasant also belonged to a community and was enmeshed in social and religious networks; he had to produce further surpluses to cover his contributions to his "ceremonial life," whether it be celebrations of births, weddings, and funerals in life's "rites of passage" or religious donations to his God or spiritual saints. This paid for his social existence in the village.

Yet subsistence and social claims on a peasant's labor and produce were not necessarily his first obligations. A German peasant and the land he occupied were at the bottom of an inverted pyramid. At each higher level, there was an authority who also had claims on the land: a landlord for rents and labor dues, a priest for tithes, a count or duke for taxes. Rents had to be paid regardless of the yearly crop yields, and payment was ensured through force—brute violence—of the lord. A German peasant's servility was emphasized every day: when he was forced to work for the lord; when he had to grind his grain at the lord's mill; when he had to pay tolls, taxes, and duties that others were excluded from; when he had to show cringing deference to the powerful lord on horseback and to his family; when he was forced to take his quarrels to the lord for decision; when he was barred from hunting in the woods or fishing in the local streams and rivers; and when he had to pay his rent *before* providing for the subsistence of his household. In the world of peasants, as a rule, wealth flowed upward to those in power. Thus, German peasants were caught in a terrible balancing act: balancing demands of their own subsistence against demands of powerful lords. And they usually were at a disadvantage against lords.

Peasants also were at a disadvantage against the silent power of the market that invaded their rural world and determined prices that they must receive for their crops or produce. A common image of peasants—apart from their being social bumpkins—was that they were shrewd bargainers, willing to quibble for hours over farthings. Behind the stereotype were people who lived on the edge of financial ruin and who were acutely sensitive to the slightest fluctuation in market prices that could give them a slight profit—or could lead to ruin and starvation. They had no choice but to quibble. Minuscule gains were real victories to be cherished in family lore.

Peasants had so much to lose and so little to gain. So many things could reduce them to beggary and possible starvation: bad weather, crop and animal diseases, the wars and feuds of their lords, bandits, personal injuries, population growth. Not surprisingly, peasants tended to be obsessively conservative, clinging to traditional ways of life and production that at least in the past had ensured survival for many but not all. A change in routine, say, a gamble with a new crop, might bring a better life, but if it failed, a peasant household could face ruin and starvation. Just as they quibbled at the marketplace, peasants were forced daily to make tough-minded, rational choices over their existence; and their peasant-reason told them to live and farm in the old, traditional way. Peasants had to construct mental hedges around their materially constricted lives to protect themselves from change and disaster. Whatever preachers told them about Christianity, or lords about social responsibilities, these messages had to be translated into peasant-talk, into their own symbols and imagery. In Niklashausen in 1476, the traditional Lenten metaphorical message of the elite that everybody must accept material poverty to find salvation came to mean in peasant-talk that woods, fields, and streams were to be held in common and that the rich were to work for wages just like the poor.

We don't really know what peasants thought—any peasant. They are largely a silent, brooding mass of humanity in history. Only occasionally do we hear their voices: when they mock and laugh at their festivals, or when they cry out in protest. We can construct a model of peasant thought, but we must rely on stray fragments of information about medieval peasants, on many incisive studies about modern-day peasants, and on our intuitions of what sort of mental structures might arise from material existence. Our model will help us make some sense of the behavior of peasants in the summer of 1476 in Niklashausen.

When German peasants gazed about their villages and the surrounding fields and woods, they saw a fixed landscape with arable fields, woods and meadows for grazing, and streams for fishing. Some marginal land might be put to the plow, but by the late fifteenth century the ruins throughout Germany of thousands of homesteads on the margin were ample testimony of the folly of farming on soil that soon was exhausted. The supply of land was therefore fixed, and so, by and large, was the food supply. And neither land nor food was equally divided among peasants and lords. This meant that in a fixed landscape with fixed resources, one person's gain was another's loss. The rich prospered only at the expense of the poor, and lords with their privileges prospered most of all. In fact, if *anybody* gained in land or food, *everybody else* was deprived by the same amount. At bottom, the peasant sense of a just society was when everybody had equal shares of the fixed resources and everybody worked the same amount. Then there would be communal harmony. Everybody would have enough food; poverty would be equally shared. This was to be one of Hans Behem's demands in his sermons.

Beneath real peasant community life, however, smoldered distrust and hostility between neighbors. A display of wealth meant that others had been deprived. One eye of the peasant was on available resources and the other on his neighbors' holdings. Land could not expand and grow; it could only be bought and sold or divided among heirs. Now, if population decreased, as it did after the Black Death in the fourteenth century, much land would become available and community tension might lessen. But if population increased, as it did after about 1450, then we would expect tensions to have sharpened between neighbors, between peasants and lords, between peasants and nonlaboring clergy, as people struggled for land and food.

Thus, prosperous peasants deflected suspicion that they had gained at the expense of their neighbors by putting their peasant virtues on public display in peasant symbols: thrift, hard work, simplicity in dress, and the saving sanctity of poverty. To flaunt wealth was to declare greed against the community. Ideally, peasants should display themselves publicly as the honest, hardworking poor. Theirs was the "culture of poverty" in Oscar Lewis' famous phrase.

Expectations for a better life among peasants were necessarily low and severely restricted. The main problem that occupied peasants was how to cope with the hardships and disaster that *must* befall them. Whatever else life offered, it would inevitably bring periodic crop failure, hail, lightning, sickness, and death. Life was a morality play of Necessity married to Fatalism.

And how were peasants to cope? Not alone as in modern, atomized society; but rather as a community—that same community that was fraught with suspicion over the unequal distribution of goods. Giving alms to the poor enriched the souls of the givers and the community as a whole. Curing the sick was often a community affair, because sickness was usually seen as a judgment from God for some wrong done in the community. Death was a public affair: a dying person, when possible, was surrounded by neighbors for comfort and support. Funerals, marriages, births, all the critical stops along the path of life, were communal affairs because they either added to the community by births, created new families and property arrangements through marriage, or reduced the community through death. Neighbors controlled deviant behavior such as adultery, wife beating, scolding, and fornication that upset the natural order of right living; norms were maintained through public laughter, public mockery, and public humiliation. All such community actions reveal to us the intense conservatism of peasant life: social expectations should remain unchanged.

Peasants, therefore, constructed mental barriers around their lives and communities to keep change—and possible disaster—at bay. They were trapped socially, economically, politically, and mentally in their own peasant world of poverty. They remained forever "peasants."

There is a sermon addressed to peasants and other workers by Cardinal Jacques de Vitry that appears in the many editions of his

*Sermones Vulgares,* or popular sermons. Jacques de Vitry was one of those thirteenth-century enthusiasts for the primitive church and the *vita apostolica* (the apostolic life) of poverty. He wrote approvingly of the new movements of voluntary poverty by urban, monied men and women such as the Franciscans and the Beguines. Jacques de Vitry took as the theme of his sermon Zachariah 13:5: *Homo agricola sum,* I am a tiller of the soil:

> *Homo agricola sum, etc.* Literally, the Holy Scriptures truly praise agriculture and manual labor, without which society would not be able to survive. After the sin of Adam, God enjoined penance on him and his sons: the Lord said, "By the sweat of your brow you will earn your bread." Therefore, those who labor with this intention that they fulfill their penance ordered by God, will be praised more and not less than those in the entire church who sing God's praises or keep vigil from night to morning. For we see many poor tillers of the soil who by the labor of their hands sustain a wife and children; and they work more than monks in their cloisters or clerics in their churches. If the intention of peasants is to fulfill the penance enjoined on them by God's injunction, then they act in love; they will acquire their temporal sustenance and attain eternal life. If, however, they are like the brute animals, and their intention is not penance but merely to eat and drink, then they will lose grace in this life and their labor will be for naught.

Labor and basic sustenance are good, he is saying, but they are good because they are lifelong penance for sin.

The desire to escape from the world, to deny the demands of flesh and blood as Lenten sermons called for, has its roots deep in Christianity. Voluntary poverty distinguished early Christian heroes such as the Desert Fathers or the monks from the rest of society. Poverty became formalized as a vow for those who devoted themselves to the religious life. Poverty was essential in order to gain spiritual riches. Christ had said as much in his praise of the meek and the poor. Only the poor could free themselves from dependence on the world in order to be dependent solely on God.

For centuries, Christians who joined religious orders took vows of poverty: monks, nuns, and by the High Middle Ages, friars. Also, all sorts of laymen and laywomen sought the sanctity of poverty without joining religious orders. What emerged in medieval Europe from the long Christian centuries was a "cult of poverty." Men and women took vows of poverty; they sought a pure Christian life of world rejection. In medieval teaching they lived ideal lives. They alone could be completely one with Christ.

But medieval Europe was largely poverty-stricken anyway. Thus, the cult of Poverty, as it was taught in sermons beyond the cloister, had great community value: it justified the poor in their labor and want, that is, it lifted from the poor (theoretically, at least) the stigma of their poverty. It also encouraged the giving of alms from the rich to the poor, as a way of lifting from the rich the curse of their prosperity. The individual possession of goods, it was widely taught, was an attack on "community." It was thus in part for the rich, the French historian Jacques le Goff has argued, that purgatory as a place for punishment of sin was invented at the end of the twelfth century. Purgation would be painful, but in the end even the rich could be saved.

The ultimate expression of a popular version of the cult of Poverty—and a measure of how deeply it penetrated to the expectations of common people—was the "bonfire of the vanities": a public bonfire into which people threw their possessions—their vanities—beyond the bare necessities. These were public demonstrations that individuals now had no claims to make on the community; they were free from the suspicion of their neighbors. The bonfires gave moral superiority to the (naturally) poor over the elite.

Those who especially propagated the cult of Poverty in late medieval Europe were the various orders of mendicant (begging) friars, as well as laymen and laywomen who tried to live like friars, the Beguines (women), the Beghards (men), and countless hermits. In speech, sermons, and actions, they exuded poverty. They put the ideal of poverty on public display throughout Europe. Everywhere people met the friar's begging bowl and his begging cry, "Brott durch Gott." Friars were not bound to a location or to their properties or estates. They moved freely from community to community. Other religious figures, such as popes, archbishops, bishops, priests, monks, and nuns, were confined to their estates, collecting rents and tithes. They could only suffer in comparison. Traveling friars often made them objects of ridicule in popular sermons.

The friars arose during the thirteenth century in part as a response to an "urban crisis" of poverty and religious neglect of the downtrodden. Poverty in the cities seemed so much worse because the poor were deprived of family, friends, and community—and there was so much wealth in the cities by comparison. So the friars were not to be confined in rural monasteries, but were to go to the cities. By the late Middle Ages, the Dominican and Franciscan orders were the most populous of all the religious orders. They had tapped into the major arteries of the medieval cultural body: they were in the new cities, they exemplified the cult of Poverty, they came to dominate the new universities and the education of the elite, and they more than anyone else propagated the new teachings of purgatory, the cult of the Virgin Mary, and the use of the rosary. As the Virgin Mary was the consummate international saint, venerated across territorial borders and social ranks, so did the traveling friars take the Virgin as their special protectress. There was even a popular legend that grew in the fifteenth century, that Mary had appeared to St. Dominic and ordered the use of the rosary through him. If an exposed nerve existed in medieval society, a friar pulled at it.

The Franciscans especially raised the question of "poverty" and kept it before people's eyes. During the thirteenth century a bitter split had opened in the Franciscan order between those who wanted to maintain the original ideals of St. Francis of complete poverty—they were called the Spirituals—and those who had made compromises with the ideal by controlling vast properties that had been given them "for their use." During the fourteenth century, the Spirituals were hounded out of existence as heretics.

But the nagging problem of the ideal of poverty remained. After 1368, in Italy, a new surge of Franciscan idealism emerged, now under the name of the Observants. The name was a self-conscious self-reference to their own especially observant regard for the rule of the order. All the great late medieval Franciscans were Observants, notably St. Bernardino of Siena and St. John Capistrano, both of whom also were famous preachers.

So, by the fifteenth century, a new split had opened in the Franciscan order, and the central issue hammered at by the Observants against their brothers, the Conventuals, was over property and poverty. In sermon after sermon, in council after council, the Observants insisted on being propertyless, hence in complete poverty, hence living the true Christian ideal. Bernardino and Capistrano portrayed and popularized their founder St. Francis as the Second Christ: for Christ, they said, had lived in complete poverty.

Sensitive laypersons also sought absolute poverty. To "find religion" or "be converted" meant to strip oneself of property and live in poverty. Some formed in groups, as many women in the Netherlands and Germany had done. They were the Beguines. Others, primarily men, became hermits. Some hermits were noted for their distinctive gray habits, which copied the Franciscans', and they were called Beghards (a corruption of the word Beguine). During the fourteenth century, Beghards particularly came under suspicion of heresy, notably by the friars who wanted to distance themselves from these lay imitators. But by the fifteenth century, the "Beghards and Beguines of voluntary poverty" (as they were known to the Inquisitors) were with few exceptions left alone by church authorities. Beghards especially were found among hermits and wandering mystics.

Hans Behem knew such a "Beghard," a mystic who lived in a cave outside Niklashausen and who apparently spoke often with young Hans. He was possibly Hans' teacher. Some chroniclers of the Niklashausen pilgrimage claimed that a mysterious friar had concocted the whole affair.

Whatever form selfless lay piety took, it meant living in poverty, away from the pomp of the world. It also meant that lay piety irresistibly inclined toward mysticism: through contemplation one may find the Sacred, the feeling of Awe, a Union with God. Ascetic mystics most often were driven by a Light Within rather than by ritual and ceremony. Hans' companion, the Beghard hermit, claimed with an air of mystery that he had lit a flame before his mountain cave to guide the common people that they not be led astray.

Strip the riches from the world. Find truth in poverty. Make a bonfire of the vanities.

It was in the sermons of wandering preachers that the cult of Poverty met the "culture of poverty." Vast numbers of sermon collections have survived, and so we know what medieval men and women were told. Of course, we do not know what they heard. Nevertheless, preaching was at the center of medieval life, whether in universities, cloisters, cities, or villages. The friars, ever since their inception in the thirteenth century, had changed the face of preaching and made it openly popular. They, more than anyone else, used down-home imagery and language, charming little stories *(exempla)* to make a moral point and change the pace of the sermon, and humor and enthusiastic delivery to hold their audiences. In fifteenth-century Germany, traveling friars drew enormous crowds of tens of thousands to their sermons.

Our textbooks, drawing on the sermons of the friars, mistakenly tell us that the medieval church was deficient in preaching and overburdened with ritual and ceremony—that is, until the Reformation, when much ritual was eliminated and reformed clerics now preached on and on . . . and on. Our view of the Reformation may be correct, but we misinterpret medieval religious life. The Dominican Savonarola, after all, in his wildly magnificent sermons found great popular response behind the facade of elitist Renaissance Florence:

Go thou to Rome and throughout Christendom; in the mansions of the great prelates and great lords there is no concern save for poetry and the oratorical art. Go thither and see, thou shalt find them all with books of the humanities in their hands and telling one another that they can guide men's souls by means of Virgil, Horace, and Cicero. . . . There thou seest the great prelates with splendid miters of gold and precious stones on their heads, and silver crosiers in hand; there they stand at the altar, decked with fine copes and stoles of brocade, chanting those beautiful vespers and masses, very slowly, and with so many grand ceremonies, so many organs and choristers, that thou are struck with amazement. . . . Men feed upon these vanities and rejoice in these pomps, and say that the Church of Christ was never so flourishing, nor divine worship so well conducted as at the present . . . likewise that the first prelates were inferior to these of our own time. . . . It is true that the founders of the church had fewer gold miters and fewer chalices, for, indeed, what few they possessed were broken up to relieve the needs of the poor. . . . What doest Thou, O Lord? Why dost Thou slumber? Arise, and come to deliver Thy Church from the hands of the devils, from the hands of the tyrants, the hands of the iniquitous prelates.

His were powerful sermons—and they brought about a revolution.

Medieval preaching was a form of public entertainment, and was often performed brilliantly. Preachers were professionals who had to hold their audiences, often for hours at a time. They knew all the rhetorical tricks of professional speakers: when to tell a story, when to analyze, when to use narrative, when to score the moral point. They knew how to engage each individual in the audience with rhetorical questions that challenged his or her complacency. They understood the rhythm of language and the emotional power of repetition and refrain.

Not everybody who preached, of course, was particularly good at it. And not everybody who wanted to preach was allowed. Preachers had to be licensed by their ecclesiastical superior, usually the local bishop. But this often was a mere technicality, because it was so difficult in medieval society, with so few police powers, to control who preached. Yet the spoken word was a powerful tool for social control—or for undermining social control. Certainly an illiterate shepherd boy such as Hans Behem could not be licensed. Who knows what he might say? Preaching was legally restricted to bishops and priests, those with "cure of souls," and to traveling friars.

Some of the best preachers of the fifteenth century were Italian friars: Savonarola, of course, but also Bernardino (now a saint) of the Observant Franciscans, and John Capistrano (also now a saint). Capistrano is especially important to my story of Hans Behem, because at least one chronicler was struck by the resemblance of Hans' preaching to Capistrano's.

When John Capistrano left his native Italy in 1451, he crossed the Alps to preach against the remnants of the Hussite heresy throughout Germany and central Europe. He was a fiery old man, sixty-five years old, austerely ascetic as was expected of one of the leaders of the Observant Franciscans, and aggressively virtuous. A chronicler from Nürnberg remembered him as "a small man . . . with meager and emaciated body, reduced to skin, veins, and bone." Capistrano drew enormous crowds wherever he preached, even though he knew no northern European languages and was forced to preach in Latin. No matter. He tells us with some pride that on one stretch of his preaching tour, between Villach and Nürnberg, he employed twenty-four different translators. Whatever was lost in translation was made up in body language and voice tone that alternated among shouting (about God's wrath) and hissing (about sin) and mellifluous tones (about the virtues of the Virgin Mary). Animated speech and wild gyrations were the characteristic style of the friars. "He preaches from two to three hours with hands and feet," sniffed Johann Busch, a confidant of the archbishop of Magdeburg, at Capistrano's mannerisms; one sermon in particular, he said, was "very long" and Capistrano "shouted terribly."

That was the view of a member of the clergy-elite. Capistrano's effect on less respectable crowds was more profound. In fact, we can follow Capistrano's trail across Germany, central Europe, and into eastern Europe, through the astonished observations of local chroniclers. We know that he stirred vast crowds to frenzy in Nürnberg,

Eichstätt, and Würzburg, in the heartland of the great Niklashausen pilgrimage. Town squares throughout Germany shuddered with the noisy dissonance of sermons, wailing, muttering, and shrieking prayers. People came not just to hear him preach, but also for some of the same reasons they flocked to pilgrimages, to be healed of their bodily ills and pains. Sick pilgrims by the thousands came to Capistrano, who touched them with the healing powers of the relics of St. Bernardino that he carried everywhere with him. The mere touch of those powerful relics—perhaps Bernardino's clothes—promised relief.

Capistrano's sermons varied from city to city and from day to day depending on local circumstances. At Nürnberg, for instance, he preached daily from July 18 to August 13, 1451. His high pulpit overlooked the marketplace, where railings separated men, women, Jews, and the sick. Jews were required to attend specific sermons throughout Europe for the purpose of conversion, a requirement imposed on them in 1434 by the Council of Basel. Important people sat in arcades built near the pulpit.

Invariably Capistrano preached on one of his favorite themes, the Virgin Mary, for, as he recalled in a personal anecdote, the Virgin had appeared to him in an apparition when he was a young man and very ill. She even gave him a drink from a silver pitcher. Ever since then he "greeted" the Virgin every time he took a drink, and he recited the *Ave Maria* before each sermon. Capistrano taught the Germans the second part of the *Ave Maria,* which until then had not been used in Germany: "Blessed Mary, Mother of God, pray for our sins, now and in the hour of our death."

Capistrano reached the climax of his sermon cycle when he drew on the prophetic, chiliastic, Joachimite tradition of the Observant Franciscans and preached on the Seven Ages of History: We are living in the Sixth Age, he said ominously, the age of poverty or the age of the mendicant friars, which began with the Second Christ, St. Francis, who was the Sixth Angel of the Apocalypse, and which will usher in the Seventh Age of the Millennium. The end is near, God is angry, and we must put away the vanities of the world and find true poverty. Gambling, usury, fashionable clothing, fancy hair styles, perfumes are all worldly vanities. And they will bring upon the entire world the terrible wrath of God. Capistrano's imagery is graphic and tactile: an impenitent sinner is like a mole whose eyes are covered with a membrane that breaks only at his death; he can see only when he dies. Newborn snakes who devour their mother's entrails are like apostate children who devour the church. Capistrano read nature as a text to find deep social connections and meaning.

The vanities of fashion, of primping before a mirror, touched a raw nerve in Capistrano and inspired his best *memento mori* performances. Fashions were useless vanities that wasted precious cloth and wealth. To adorn what? Capistrano lifted a skull high for all to see and cried out: "Here is your mirror. Look in and see your reflection. Where is that nose that inhaled such pleasing odors? Where is that hair that once delighted you? Where is that tongue that slandered? Worms have devoured all." In Vienna, he lashed out at fashionable neck ruffs, and likened them to the spiked collars worn by guard dogs in Abruzzi who protected sheep from wolves: "Are you women here in Vienna afraid of wolves? Take my advice: I will pray to God that the wolves spare you, and you give me your ruffs for the church and the poor." In the end was Death, the naked skull, the great leveler of popes and princes, which reduced all to the same mixture of worms and slime.

Now came the moment of truth for the audience: the bonfire of the vanities. Capistrano challenged the crowd to rid themselves of their vanities, their gaming boards, their dice, their neckerchiefs, their headdresses, their wigs, their pointed shoes, and to throw them into a massive bonfire. All across Europe, wherever John Capistrano preached, great bonfires consumed the vanities of the world. Chroniclers in Nürnberg were in awe of the high shooting flames that left an eerie blue cloud over the city, and which burned, they said, three thousand checkerboards, forty thousand dice sets, and wagonloads of padded hats, doublets with slashed sleeves, hairpieces, and pointed shoes.

As social drama, the sermons and bonfires drove home the social doctrine of the equality of all believers and the vanity of rank, status, and wealth. This merely reinforced what peasants already knew to be social justice. Hans Behem preached the same message a generation later.

Sometime during the late summer or fall of 1476, an anonymous poet wrote a long piece of doggerel about the events he had witnessed surrounding the great pilgrimage to Niklashausen during May, June, and July of that year. The poet probably was a cleric and a member of the bishop of Würzburg's household. His jogging rhythms and rhymes are impossible to reproduce, but the sense of his opening twenty-five lines is clear, that the Virgin Mary instructed Hans Behem to call for a pilgrimage to Niklashausen to preach Lenten sermons on the bonfire of the vanities:

> It all happened in the year after the birth of Christ, fourteen hundred and seventy-six. No man, no matter how old, had ever seen such a strange affair that I will in truth tell. A drummer let himself be fooled by deceitful cunning while in a clearing in the woods near Niklashausen—as all men and women know. To him appeared the Mother of God and spoke with great respect: "If you wish to do my will, then you will soon burn your drum, and preach to all the folk, and tell them that they should make a pilgrimage to Niklashausen; and they should take off their false braids and their pointed shoes and their neckerchiefs. They are vain things." That happened during Lent.

Hans' drum, his prized possession, was a vanity and was committed to the flames. But he now had his license to preach, not from the bishop, but from heaven, from the Mother of God. She would tell him what to say when the pilgrims arrived at Niklashausen. And they most certainly would come. At Niklashausen pilgrims would be able to hear the Word of God, through the Virgin Mary and her chosen shepherd.

On Good Friday, April 12, Lent was almost over. That evening, throughout Germany, all fires were doused in churches and hearths. The world was in darkness.

Then on Saturday, preceding Easter, new fires were lit. In the church was the Easter candle that was used to rekindle all the lights throughout the church. In the marketplace before the church doors a great bonfire was lit. In some parts of Germany the bonfire was on a hilltop and villagers competed with each other to see who could make the greatest blaze. People brought their own sticks of oak or walnut or beech, which they charred in the bonfire, and then returned home to burn them in their hearths accompanied by prayers to protect their houses from fire, lightning, and hail. Every household began Easter with a new fire from the common bonfire. This was a time of renewal, a time of joy and hope from the ashes of the Paschal fires.

Throughout upper Franconia and Bavaria, villagers made a straw-man named Judas, which they burned in the churchyard on Easter Sunday. A whole village contributed wood for the pyre on which Judas perished. The charred sticks were kept and planted in fields on May Day, following *Walpurgisnacht,* to preserve the crops from blight and mildew. The ashes of peasant fires had magical qualities that ensured rebirth and fertility.

Lent, at last, was over.

# IV

## *Walpurgisnacht*

Easter Sunday was followed by the
seven weeks of Easter that led to
Pentecost (the seventh Sunday) and a
celebration of the descent of the Holy
Spirit on the apostles after the
resurrection of Christ. In 1476, Pentecost fell on June 2. Between Easter and
Pentecost were many other celebrations
and feast days. In Germany, for example, was celebrated the Feast of St.
Walburga, or *Walpurgisnacht,* on April
30, the eve of May Day. Walburga was
an eighth-century Anglo-Saxon nun
and missionary to Franconia, particularly to Bischofsheim on the Tauber,
just south of Niklashausen. Her bones
were "translated" (that is, moved) on
April 30—which became her feast day
—sometime during the 870s to Eichstätt, where her brother Willibald had

been bishop. Ever since then an oily liquid has oozed out of the rock on which her tomb rests, and has been renowned among pilgrims for its great healing power. St. Walburga was revered not only in the Tauber Valley and Franconia but also throughout much of Germany as a protectress against plague and hunger. From its inception, her feast day (or rather night) was bound to the old pagan holiday of May Day (May 1) that celebrated the beginning of summer and the expulsion of witches.

On *Walpurgisnacht* in 1476 great peasant bonfires were lit yet again, but this time to drive away witches, screaming unheard and unseen through the cool night air. It was an emotionally mixed feast day: joyful, hopeful against disease and famine, yet portentous with witches and the threat of a summer season of pestilence and hunger. It heralds for us the ominous onset of the pilgrimage to Niklashausen, where pilgrims hoped to find the healing balm of Hans Behem.

Shortly after *Walpurgisnacht,* in early May 1476, large groups of people began to congregate in the small village of Niklashausen, called there by the peasant shepherd, Hans Behem. From the beginning, people witnessed his miraculous powers: during the first days of May, God lifted his wrath from Germany and sent warm winds to melt the deep snows that had piled in drifts over frozen fields. Hans' prayers to the Virgin had eased God's anger. Word spread rapidly throughout Germany—by what means we do not know—about the miraculous vision and powers of Hans, the "holy youth." From far and wide, "the common folk" *(das gemeyn folck* as chroniclers called them) came to Niklashausen. They traveled alone, in small groups, but most often in great "troops" (chroniclers were at a loss for any other word), and they carried great banners and gigantic candles that only three or four men could lift.

"All Germany seemed to be in commotion," wrote Georg Widman many years later in his dramatic account of the pilgrimage. Stableboys left their horses, taking the bridles with them, he said; reapers left their reaping, carrying their scythes; women ceased haying in the middle of their fields, and came to Niklashausen with their rakes;

wives left their husbands, husbands left their wives, children left their parents. Common people from all over central and south Germany—from Saxony, the Rhineland, Hesse, Thuringia, Swabia, Bavaria, and, of course, Franconia—simply dropped what they were doing and went to Niklashausen.

Widman insinuated that the pilgrims were attracted by cheap wine from roadside taverns and the promiscuous sex in the barns and the fields where the pilgrims slept. His analysis may betray elitist, clerical fantasies and disdain for common folk, but he was correct about the type of people who became pilgrims. With few exceptions they were peasants and peasant-artisans. What was so frightening to authorities—those whom Widman spoke for—was that these people took to the road to Niklashausen and did not ask anybody's permission, not from their landlords to leave work, not from their priests to go on a pilgrimage. Social rank and obligations just seemed to dissolve.

Secular and religious authorities in Mainz, Wertheim, and Würzburg soon learned of the spontaneous pilgrimage. All had some responsibility for the village of Niklashausen and its priest, and they were touchy about any mass gathering. Throughout Germany there had already been many sporadic popular uprisings against landlords and the clergy. Now, in May, a new popular movement had begun, a whirlwind of people was gathering in the Tauber Valley around the small village of Niklashausen, and the authorities were alarmed.

In late May or early June, several weeks after the pilgrimage had begun, Count Johann of Wertheim wrote to Archbishop Dieter to inform him of the pilgrimage. He had not yet heard of Hans Behem, but he had heard reports that many people had experienced visions and apparitions. What was actually happening and what it all meant, admitted the count, was a mystery. He asked in his letter that someone besides himself—someone with spiritual authority—investigate the extraordinary happenings in Niklashausen. If any "injustices" occurred, the count said, then he would act with force, but for the time being he preferred to do nothing. Why? Because, he added, the pilgrimage—no matter how strange it was—had been very profitable for him and his subjects, who supplied food, shelter, and other goods to the swarm of pilgrims. The count concluded with the sanctimony of a chamber of commerce president: the pilgrimage, after all, did seem honorable because it was called in the name of the Virgin Mary, the Queen of Heaven.

By early June, a clearer picture of the pilgrimage had begun to take focus in the minds of authorities. Archbishop Dieter of Mainz now knew that a youthful layman named Hans Behem was at the center of all the commotion, and that Hans belonged to the diocese of Würzburg. On June 13, the archbishop wrote to the bishop of Würzburg, Rudolph von Sherenberg, to tell him that the Youth was the topic of conversation "far and wide and everywhere"; the common folk believed in his visions and now were flocking to Niklashausen to touch him, to hear him preach, and, yes, even to hear him foretell the future. "This pseudo-prophet," as Archbishop Dieter called him, preached to the ignorant masses doctrines that were repugnant to the orthodox Catholic faith: what more could upset the little boat of the Divine Peter than these ill winds from Niklashausen?

Thus, Archbishop Dieter called for action. Hans must be stopped before he infected all of Germany. In turgid, bureaucratic Latin, the first official actions against Hans Behem were now ordered. Archbishop Dieter granted authority over the Niklashausen affair to the jurisdiction of Bishop Rudolph of Würzburg. Bishop Rudolph was ordered to crack down on the "pseudo-prophet," to prohibit Hans from preaching, to inquire carefully into such errors promulgated by him, and to discover who his companions, associates, and followers were—and to root them out with his troops. No one was to preach without the bishop's license. No one was to celebrate mass in the church of Niklashausen without the bishop's permission. No one was to preach, speak, or act in any way that was against the canons of the church or that disturbed the peace. Archbishop Dieter fully realized that they were all caught in the forming vortex of an ominous mass movement. Where would it all end?

To a fifteenth-century German observer and political official, a rapidly formed pilgrimage such as the one in Niklashausen set off alarm bells. Time was out of joint: a boy shepherd had become a prophet; social rank disintegrated as the world became inside out, upside down; masses of people shed their goods (their "vanities") to find the true poverty of Christ.

Normal time and festival time had always been separated by specific dates, ceremonies, and rituals throughout the year. Carnival ended on Shrove Tuesday, Lent ended at Easter. Now there was a confusion of time. The upside-down world of Carnival broke through the barriers of Lent, and Lent broke through the barriers of Easter and flowed into Pentecost. Hans Behem, the Carnival drummer, had carried with him to Niklashausen the upside-down social world of Carnival and the Lenten message of self-denial and salvation through poverty. For Hans, enchanted time did not end when it was supposed to, but continued into the summer. The heavens had opened up and had spoken through young Hans for weeks at a time that defied the church calendar.

Peasants by the thousands went to Niklashausen. They seem to have been driven like lemmings by mysterious forces. The pilgrimage to Niklashausen, however, was not a unique event, but rather part of a late fifteenth-century pattern in Germany of many spontaneous, frenetic pilgrimages. German peasants so desperately wanted . . . something . . . but what?

Salvation. They wanted salvation in their material and spiritual lives. German peasants were pushed about on the stage of history by powerful, impersonal forces—demography, economic trends, disease, and so forth—which they could never fully comprehend and could explain only by an appeal to the enchanted world. Hans Behem was their spokesman. His dreams and fantasies were their dreams and fantasies; his anger was theirs. That is why they listened to him. We must try to penetrate their physical and mental world if we are to make sense of the pilgrimage to Niklashausen and of Hans' cry for material and spiritual salvation.

The Tauber Valley in the 1470s had much empty pastureland for Hans' animals. We may guess that Hans saw daily the remains of old homesteads and fields that had long since been abandoned. Young forests now grew where arable fields used to be. Germany by 1476 was relatively empty, certainly when compared with Germany in the early fourteenth century.

Since the fourteenth century, great changes in the population of Germany (in fact, of all Europe) had taken place. The story of the Black Death coming to Europe during 1348–1350 is well known. What we must remind ourselves is that the disease flared up constantly for the next three and one-half centuries and periodically ravaged populations. The destinies of all people in late medieval Germany were determined by the blind reproduction of plague bacteria. For the first century of the disease, outbreaks were largely pandemic, devastating whole populations throughout Europe. After 1349, the population of Germany dropped drastically, leaving great empty lands. After about 1450, however, the plague tended to be less virulent and was largely confined to local outbreaks. It also became a disease more of towns and cities than of the countryside. After about 1450, population slowly began to increase. Germany still had much empty land, but a growing population in the countryside began to push relentlessly against available resources. Although disease and famine still stalked the lives of people, the forces of fertility were winning out at last against the forces of death.

The release of population pressure after 1349 had profound effects in the German countryside and towns. Much land suddenly became available and jobs for skilled labor opened in the towns. The great impersonal forces of history now favored workers and lesser peasants who worked for others—anybody who lived by wages. Rents fell, as lords tried desperately to entice peasants to take up holdings. Wages rose, as employers competed for labor. Food prices fell, as did the prices of commodities. For about a hundred years, between 1349 and c.1450, wealth was redistributed downward. High wages, low rents, low cost of living. A carpenter in Würzburg in 1387, for example, could purchase with his wages for *one day* 30 kilograms (or about 66 pounds) of grain. Nothing like this had happened before in medieval Europe and would not be repeated until the modern industrial, welfare state.

The benefits of the fall in population for skilled laborers was obvious. But for peasants it was a mixed picture. Prosperous peasants who had to hire workers, no doubt, suffered by paying high wages to produce grain in a falling market. Landless peasants who had only their labor to sell prospered—but only relative to their former condition. They were still poor peasants. For most peasants of the middling sort who farmed their own land, but under a lord, life may have only slightly improved. Their rents (however they might be calculated: in money, labor, or produce) fell, but so did the market price for their produce. The rise in wages might help them, but only if they hired themselves out for work beyond their own fields. The central economic issue of peasant lives was not wages but credit. The peasants needed to borrow to survive from sowing time to harvest, and their landlords were the natural lenders, and, therefore, their natural enemies.

Following the Black Death, peasants abandoned marginal land and moved either to prime, arable sites or to towns and cities where wages were high and opportunities great. Of course, hazards of disease were also greater in the towns and cities, which were little more than disease pits. Yet the peasants came. In the towns peasants saw their chance to escape the misery of peasant life—miserable even in favorable circumstances. Urban population numbers held fairly steady but only because of huge infusions of people from the countryside. And much of the countryside became empty. Before the plague there were about 170,000 settlements of varying sizes in Germany. By about 1450, around 40,000 of those settlements had disappeared. They were turned to pasture or to woods, and have since been known to German historians by the wonderfully desolate-sounding word *Wüstungen,* the wastelands of the lost villages of Germany.

Powerful economic forces had favored wage workers and peasants for a century, but, with the exception of those who fled to the towns, it did not change their rank in society. Lords remained lords, peasants remained peasants. At first lords lost heavily on their lands, but during the fifteenth century, they tried new strategies to make a profit with a minimum of labor. Some planted forests to harvest wood. Some changed their crops from labor-intensive cereal grains to grapes in wine vineyards that still fetched high prices on the market and required only seasonal labor. Others turned to raising stock, especially pigs, whose prices also remained high; animals required only empty land and the labor of a herdsman, perhaps a mere boy like Hans Behem.

So by about 1450, the economic landscape of medieval Germany had altered considerably. Not as much grain was grown and more land was used to raise animals. Much land seemed empty, but empty only of people. Land was still occupied by animals and the rights of lords. Again during the fifteenth century famine was a specter of peasant life.

Lords were getting the upper hand by the 1450s, '60s and '70s, in part because of their strategies in a depleted labor market, in part because of the gradual recovery of population from the ravages of plague. Population grew after the mid-fifteenth century—slowly, to be sure, but enough to favor the lords and employers against peasants and wageworkers.

A chronicler from Erfurt in 1483 looked back with relief when he recorded that "within these twenty years there has not been any real pestilence; and seldom is there a couple but they have eight, nine, or ten children." Peasants no doubt thanked St. Walburga for her help in staying the hand of God from bringing pestilence.

Those children may have been a blessing to a peasant couple, but they were a curse to the peasantry as a whole. Rising population meant a reversal of earlier trends. Prices remained depressed, but only relatively, for after about 1450, wages began to nose-dive. Whatever fragmentary evidence we have shows that laborers' wages bought fewer and fewer goods. Our Würzburg carpenter may still have received the equivalent of 30 kilos of grain for a day's wage in 1450, but each year thereafter he received less. Landlords reasserted their old rights over the peasantry, and demanded that labor services be done as they had been under the "old law." Tolls, taxes, and duties were imposed by all higher authorities.

Peasants after 1450 were still far better off than their ancestors in the early thirteenth century, but they did not know how their distant ancestors lived. They knew how their fathers and grandfathers lived, and knew that lords were demanding more now than before. They did not have the perspective to articulate what we can today, that powerful lords and princes in Germany were consolidating their territories; they were flexing their economic muscle against their subjects by imposing the "old laws" of tolls, taxes, duties, and labor services.

Peasant memories of "old laws" were different. Their immediate memories told them that their fathers did not have to pay these impositions. Their distant, mythical memories told them of a time "in the beginning" when there were no lords and everybody worked as equals. "When Adam plowed and Eve spun wool, who then was the lord?" was the peasant dictum throughout Europe.

From the mid-fifteenth century onward, bitterness in the German countryside deepened. Many peasant rebellions flared up especially in southern Germany during the second half of the fifteenth century and continued sporadically until the great conflagration of 1525.

It is in this general context of lords rebounding against peasants that Hans Behem preached, calling for a pilgrimage of peasants to Niklashausen. He, through the Virgin Mary, through God Himself, would explain to them why they suffered so.


Hans and the peasants who went to Niklashausen did not have the luxury of economic historians such as Wilhelm Abel explaining in brilliant detail the dynamics of population, wages, rents, and prices that push people about like puppets. A modern interpretation that explains the dynamics of history in terms of "impersonal forces," as I have done, leads to fatalism—like peasant-thought—but a benign fatalism because nobody is responsible for misery (except blind bacteria) and nobody bears guilt. Fifteenth-century peasant explanations of the historical process also led to fatalism, but it was a vicious fatalism, because it led only to individual and collective guilt.

Medieval people were caught in a mental trap, one that ensured that they would feel anxiety, divine condemnation, and guilt. In order to comprehend how they thought, how they *felt,* about existence, we must mentally strip ourselves of those assumptions about the world that we most take for granted: our explanations of causation.

When we try to make sense of why things happen—*anything,* from the weather to economic inflation—we turn to a "natural" explanation, that is, we regard phenomena as consequences of orderly, rational laws of nature. Most of us do not need to explain things by turning to a supernatural force, such as a god who plays by arbitrary rules, or, at least, by rules known only to it.

The best educated of medieval people also argued that things happened by natural causation, but by "natural" they meant something different from our definition. Nature (hence that which is "natural") for them was not something apart from a supernatural force, that is, God, but rather was under the control and guidance of that same force. The law of nature was for them simply the law of God: God does nothing contrary to the laws of nature—which would be our definition of a miracle—but is directly responsible for everything that happens in nature even if goes against normal expectations. Thus, for medieval intellectuals the miraculous and the normal tended to be the same thing: something merely seems a miracle because we do not understand the mind of God.

Medieval men—the best and the brightest at the universities—could equate the miraculous and the normal in large part because they had so little understanding of what was normal. They had no idea what were the "natural causes" (in our sense) of the simplest things in nature: wind, rain, weather. For complex phenomena, such as disease, they of course had no means to detect microscopic, harmful organisms. For the best educated, then, a miracle was merely the higher law of God. A miracle was "natural," that is, it was still a law of nature, but one that humans did not understand. A miracle, therefore, was God revealing Himself in nature. It was something to be held in awe. This was a perfectly rational deduction from the dual premises that God is the Author of all nature, and that we do not comprehend God.

While medieval intellectuals understood existence in academic syllogisms, less-educated men and women found the world and their own existence even more of a wonder: indeed, existence was a perpetual and constant miracle perpetrated by a wide array of spiritual forces from the enchanted realm. For common folk the question was always the same: *who* made this happen?—for example, rain, hail, disease, conception, rising prices, lower wages—rather than the more "scientific" question, *how* did this happen? Who is responsible for those powerful winds? Who made my cow ill? Who brought the rain at harvest time? Whose greed has changed the market price for grain? Who brought the warm winds in May 1476 to melt the heavy winter snows? Who?

The answer to the question "Who?" was not obvious to medieval folk, for their world was a sort of "chaos" of conflicting supernatural wills. Very little in life or nature could be predicted. Religious rituals and ceremonies, the blessing of the fields, the bonfires, the all-pervading and bewildering variety of peasant magic, the specified periods of enchanted time, all could help tame the chaos—but the world was still chaos. God certainly controlled everything from moment to moment by Himself or through a myriad of invisible saints, but Satan and his army of evil servants were also loose in the air. Was something harmful, such as a disease, sent by God or by Satan? Either one could be responsible: God, because of his wrathful punishment for sin; Satan, in order to possess and destroy people's bodies. In fact, it did not matter who brought disease and misery, because sick individuals necessarily bore the *guilt* of their own illnesses: people who suffer must either be sinful and an affront to God, or in the grips of Satan and thus weak-willed and possessed of evil.

The physical misery of medieval people is one clue to help us understand much of their behavior, which seems at times to be so bizarre, so frenzied. We know a great deal about medieval diet and can be reasonably certain that most people suffered from nutritional deficiencies. They suffered, often and painfully, from digestive problems, worms and other parasites, skin sores, bad teeth and gums, sore eyes, throbbing joints, festering leg and foot sores, and the like. Doctors of medicine could do very little to help and were rightly suspected of being quacks. Most people, rich and poor, hurt, and there was no sure relief from pain.

*Who* was responsible for this physical misery? Few people thought that a physical problem had a physical cause. Rather, disease and pain had spiritual, moral causes brought on by some supernatural power for a reason. What was the intention of this supernatural power, whether God and His saints or Satan and his minions? Surely, people reasoned, the harmful actions of God or Satan must be related to our own bad behavior: we suffer because we have sinned. The world may have been a sort of chaos, but it contained an underlying, relentless logic: to suffer physical illness was to be guilty. Everybody suffered physically. Everybody was guilty.

The sick must be possessed by evil spirits, because Satan, as all knew, had power over the bodies of men. People constantly fought against devil possession, and at the onset of every illness they lost the battle—only to find God's mercy at their recovery. Later generations in the sixteenth and seventeenth centuries would deflect their guilt and fear of possession onto witches. But not yet, not in 1476.

Intense and massive guilt manifested itself everywhere during the fifteenth century—in art, in popular movements, in sermons, everywhere. Evil clearly was winning the war over souls.

Evil, then, was not some abstraction, not some vague, academic description of bad behavior. Rather, it was like so much else in the late medieval popular imagination, something concrete, something that one could see and touch and smell. Evil caused physical harm, every bit as much as a falling branch or flooding waters. People felt the physical presence of evil spirits in the air, in animals, in deformed humans. A gust of wind could be the breath of Satan. Church bells at a person's death drove away the evil spirits in the air ready to snatch the soul as it slithered from the open mouth of the deceased. Holy water scattered around the bed of a dying person, or consecrated bread left on a windowsill, warded off demons. Everything had a physical, tactile presence. A "physical" evil spirit or a "physical" divine spirit made a physical imprint on bodies. Moral and physical problems were the same thing.

If physical illness was a moral problem, the solution to illness was moral cleansing. The question asked by most people was not *how* can I be cured, but *who* in the spiritual realm will cure me. Who will drive out the evil spirits? The best cures came from the best doctors of the soul, and the best doctor of the soul was God Himself. But direct access to God was difficult. A supplicant needed spiritual helpers, or intercessors, who could plead with God on his or her behalf—just as the best way for a common person to approach a temporal lord for favors was through his household servants. God's household was filled with men and women whom He favored, the saints in heaven. But the one with the greatest influence—few people really doubted this—was the Mother of God, Mary.

And where could one find these saints? At their shrines, to which the supplicant made a pilgrimage with a contrite heart. People assumed that the actual saints and the Virgin were spiritually present at their own shrines and would hear the cries of the pilgrim-supplicants. The benevolent spirit of a saint pierced the murky fog of demons and cordoned off a territory of light surrounding his or her shrine. The closer one came to the shrine, the greater its power to cure and to cleanse.

Pilgrim-supplicants eventually had to return to their own homes, but there were other shrines, other pilgrimages that they could make. At least temporarily pilgrims entered the hallowed space surrounding a shrine and relieved two pressing problems: physical illness and oppressive guilt. It was only temporary. Darkness and evil always seemed to prevail.

If earthly life was a losing battle against the forces of darkness, would death be any better? Would the misery of existence find relief? Perhaps for a few. That is all that had been promised. Preachers were especially fond of quoting from Scripture that many are called but few are chosen. Most of humanity would be damned to hell to suffer forever in ways usually described in vivid, gruesome, physical detail. Of course, earlier, during the thirteenth century, the church had accepted a relatively new concept of purgatory—as a physical place—which no doubt eased some of the fears of sinners; the torments of purgatory at least had a time limit and led to salvation.

Many devices were used in the late Middle Ages to help those in purgatory, and a good measure of people's obsessive concern for relief from purgatorial torments were the many chantries established throughout Germany to provide for perpetual prayers to the heavens for the souls of the deceased; the many "brotherhoods" in every church to provide mutual support and mutual prayers; and the enormous upsurge in pilgrimages in part to seek "indulgences" for dead souls. The medieval mentality of guilt and longing for salvation led directly to the pilgrimage trail.

The Virgin Mary told Hans Behem to summon people to make a pilgrimage to her shrine at Niklashausen. For people to make a pilgrimage was not new. However, it was a new phenomenon in Germany that obscure pilgrimage sites such as Niklashausen should become popular, if only briefly. During the fifteenth century many such sites throughout Germany blazed with pilgrim intensity for a few months, only to see the fiery enthusiasm flicker out. Pilgrims were drawn by the word of a miraculous vision or a miraculous event such as a bleeding statue or bleeding sacrament host. This was the case, for example, in a series of pilgrimages in 1475 and again in 1487 to the small German village of Wilsnack, where massive numbers of pilgrims gathered after hearing reports of a "bleeding host." Alarmed authorities tried to discourage pilgrims from Wilsnack, but to little avail. In the diocese of Würzburg, brief pilgrimages had also formed at Deitelbach after a man was healed by a statue of the Virgin, and at Tynbach after a reported miracle, and even at the chapel dedicated to Mary in Würzburg itself.

Rulers of society everywhere feared spontaneous pilgrimages because of the potentially explosive nature of large gatherings of the lower orders. Medieval authorities perhaps intuited what we now know: supernatural visions tend to occur at points of great social or economic stress; and spontaneous pilgrimages to relieve pain and suffering also tend to raise social and economic grievances under the cover of highly charged, religious language. Such spontaneous pilgrimages, replete with visions and sightings of the Virgin, were to be repeated in nineteenth-century Latin America, and often turned into protorevolutionary movements against colonialism and capitalism.

But we miss the emotional drive of what pilgrims felt, the wild dynamism of spontaneous medieval pilgrimages, if we see pilgrimages merely as an irrational facade for real, rational social and economic wants. Throughout the history of Christian pilgrimage, pilgrims saw themselves in a unique condition as a wanderers in the world, cut off from the life of society and economic livelihood. As wanderers they showed contempt for the world and all its goods. The true pilgrim entered the cult of Poverty and found relief for misery and guilt.

However, pilgrims did not wander aimlessly. They traveled to a specific site, hoping to find special healing powers—whether from the vials of oil from Walburga's tomb in Eichstätt or from the water at Lourdes, France—to heal them physically and spiritually and to cleanse away sin. The pilgrimage trail was the way to material and spiritual salvation. Because pilgrimages healed the sick in spirit as well as the sick in body, they became absorbed into the system of penances administered by the church. At least this is the official, and officially historical, version.

Pilgrimage, in fact, is a much more interesting phenomenon. Pilgrimage sites indeed were holy places, and they all had one thing in common: they were the site of a past miracle which could recur at any moment. At a pilgrimage shrine a breach had opened in the veil that separates heaven and earth, a tear in the fabric that would not be closed. It was as if a heavenly ray—here we must imagine, with medieval artists, a ray breaking through clouds—were shining from heaven on a specific earthly location. Anybody who entered the holy spotlight partook directly of the miraculous, for the light was filled with the unseen presence of a saint, or Christ, or the Virgin. Within this heavenly ray, a pilgrim could find the healing powers that only God, His family, and His companions could provide.

The point of a pilgrimage, of course, was, and is, *movement:* from the mundane to the mysterious, from normal time and space to enchanted time and space, from homes and familiar surroundings to the unfamiliar "light" of a holy place. This is an act of free choice. Pilgrims choose to go, to free themselves from the sins and pollution of the world. What we must understand, and feel along with the pilgrims, is that pilgrimage is an act of liberation, not just from sin, but also from the everyday social bonds that hold people in ranks of obedience. A pilgrimage may be made without the sanction of clergy; and grace may be received at a holy site directly from heaven without the intercession of clergy. We should not be surprised that bishops and princes were suspicious of pilgrimages. There was something inherently populist, anarchical, and even anticlerical about them—especially if one suddenly sprang up at an obscure, underpoliced location.

Thus, at the word of a miracle or apparition or vision—a mysterious opening of heaven to mortals—people from far and wide flocked to the holy site. They were temporarily freed from their worldly bonds of rank and status. In order to find grace at the sacred shrine, all must find true humility and freedom from the world. At a holy shrine, in the holy light, pilgrims were consciously "leveled" in rank and status: pilgrims simplified their dress and behavior; titles of rank disappeared; pilgrims called each other "brother" and "sister." They shared a profound sense of community—and they shared their goods and provisions. More often than not, the sacred and the profane were mingled together in a crazy-quilt atmosphere of joy, solemnity, and carnival. The normal restraints of the world were loosened in a festival of otherworldliness.

One modern anthropologist, Victor Turner, describes pilgrimage as a "liminoid" experience. This is an ugly word that describes an experience that is like, but not the same as, a "liminal" experience or a "rite of passage." A rite of passage is a ritual, usually sanctioned by society, that accompanies a person's change in status, location, or age,

61

such as a male's "coming of age" ritual that marks the transition from boyhood to manhood. The transition usually takes place in three stages: separation from normal society, passage through the margin or "limen" of social categories, and finally reintegration into a new place in society. While one is in a liminal state, one belongs nowhere and fits in no category; a male in a liminal stage of passage to manhood, for example, is neither a boy nor a man. And, briefly, he is even beyond socially defined "time," that is, he is "timeless."

Pilgrimages are like that—but not the same. Pilgrims choose to go through their experience; they are not required by social convention. The "rite of passage" (that is, to be cleansed of sin and brought to a new spiritual life) is repeatable. One may go on pilgrimages as often as one wishes and be continually "renewed." Thus a pilgrim is largely *outside* social control. In fact, a pilgrimage may be antisocial rather than socially integrating.

Yet, as in a genuine rite of passage, pilgrims enter a state of sacred time and sacred space. They enter the ray of light from heaven where they may be in awe of the Holy or the Sacred. Pilgrims enter the holy space, shorn of status and rank, to find salvation for themselves and their loved ones, to heal their souls from sin and guilt, and to heal their bodies from pain. A pilgrim is integrated with the Holy, not with society, which is why a spontaneous pilgrimage can be so dangerous for rulers: pilgrims are responsible to no one but God.

That sounds very abstract. Medieval people, in fact, preferred something more tangible and concrete. What exactly could pilgrims get at a pilgrimage shrine—besides souvenirs? They could obtain a papal indulgence in the form of a piece of paper on which was promised remission of punishment in purgatory for sins committed. The usual length of remission was forty days. One could also receive an indulgence for loved ones already suffering in purgatory. According to theologians an indulgence was given only after the sins of the penitent pilgrim were forgiven through confession and contrition. But this often was a mere technicality.

At the popular level, certainly during the fifteenth century, indulgence meant that a pilgrim could find forgiveness of his sins *automatically* by visiting certain pilgrimage shrines or churches, or by doing certain good deeds such as contributing toward the construction of a church. The popular conception was not necessarily wrong. It merely pushed a fuzzy theological concept of indulgences to its logical, unintended limits. People wanted salvation and they were not about to let mere theologians stand in their way.

Indulgences were at the heart of the medieval penitential system, which in turn was at the heart of the church's reason-for-being. The church, through the pope, acted as a mediator between heaven and earth. It dispensed God's special favors, or grace, and it absolved people from their sins against God. When a person committed a sin, he or she had to confess it to a priest who then imposed the appropriate punishment (or "penance"). After penance was performed, the priest then absolved the penitent of his or her sin. What is important for us to see in the penitential system is the exclusive role of the clergy, whether priest, bishop, or pope.

From the eleventh century, the doctrine of "indulgence" emerged whereby the pope—and the pope alone—had the power to release a sinner from the imposed penance by granting an indulgence. The sinner was then freed from the temporal punishments for his or her sins. How much punishment was remitted? All, if the sinner received a plenary (or full) indulgence; part of it, if he or she received a partial indulgence.

The theory that supported this papal *largesse* over sin and redemption was fully articulated by theologians during the thirteenth century. The argument goes this way: the church has a treasury of merits and good deeds; here are stored the merits and good deeds of Christ, the Virgin Mary, and all the saints, living and dead; the pope alone has access to this wonderful treasury and may dip into it to use some of those stored merits to pay the debt of sinners. Thus payment from the treasury is not so much a remission of a sin (or debt)—which implies forgiveness or pardon—as it is a repayment from another source of what was owed. That is what Thomas Aquinas had said. The controlling idea of the argument is that a debt is vicariously satisfied. And it came to include satisfaction of punishment in purgatory as well as temporal penance. What is so miraculous about this treasury is that the funds deposited, that is, merits and good works, are infinite. The treasury will never run dry. Never.

Given the notion of an infinite treasury to pay off debts of temporal sinners, we may easily imagine the enormous pressure on the keeper of the treasury, the pope, to release the funds. Gradually, popes relented to the incessant clamoring for indulgences. Pope Boniface VIII declared the year 1300 to be a Jubilee Year and granted an indulgence to anybody who came to Rome. Hundreds of thousands of penitents made the trip. Other Jubilee years were declared, and by the mid-fifteenth century, a Jubilee was ordained to be held every twenty-five years. During the fourteenth century, popes delegated their power over the treasury to archbishops and bishops throughout Europe. Thus, penitents needed only to go to their local bishop for an indulgence, which was just as good as going to Rome. In fact, by the fourteenth century, popes had granted their remarkable powers not only to other officials of the church but also to various *places* such as churches and shrines. One had only go to a local pilgrimage shrine to obtain a papal indulgence. The treasury, after all, was infinite. There were enough merits for *everybody*.

Even the smallest churches were able to ask for and obtain—for a fee—power over indulgences. For a small, financially strapped church to become an indulgence site, hence a pilgrimage site, was a great financial boon. Income from offerings of the pilgrims as well as from providing food and housing raised the incomes of pastors and rebuilt many a church in Europe. The obscure village church of Niklashausen received its power to grant indulgences from Innocent VI in 1354, and thus became a pilgrimage site.

For a year or so before Hans Behem called for his pilgrimage, there probably had been much preaching and common talk throughout Germany concerning indulgences, because 1475 was a Jubilee year. Preachers no doubt focused attention on salvation, the doctrine of purgatory, and the promise of a papal indulgence for those who went to Rome. When Hans began to preach, however, he claimed that he—not the pope—had power over salvation, that forgiveness could be had in Niklashausen rather than in Rome, and that purgatory was an invention of the clergy.

Niklashausen, therefore, in 1476 was the best pilgrimage site of all, because the Virgin actively was working miracles and remitting *all* sins. People could ensure their salvation by having all debts paid for sin. People who spent their lives haggling over pennies and farthings in the marketplace, who knew the return of their labor in the field and in their lord's hall, who calculated every tax, toll, and duty on their daily well-being—these same people could also calculate their savings in indulgences for their sins and reckon the necessary costs to get into heaven. Salvation could be calculated as well as the prices of chickens, bread, and beans. And a pilgrimage to Niklashausen was a bargain.

Why did people go on pilgrimages? Obviously for many reasons: to cure bodily ills, to find salvation, to relieve guilt, to partake of the Holy in a state of divine poverty. For many old folks, usually men and usually old priests who were ill and awaiting death, it was customary to go on a pilgrimage naked down to a loincloth. With outstretched arms before a shrine they emulated Christ on the Cross before His death.

Pilgrimages also attracted an extraordinarily large number of young Germans in their teens. Between the years 1455 and 1459, thousands of German children between the ages of eight and eighteen made a series of long pilgrimages to Mont St. Michel in Normandy. They traveled in troops of several hundred, carrying before them the banner of St. Michael. The children came from all over Germany, from Lübeck, Eichstätt, Ulm, Halle, Regensburg . . . everywhere. Town chroniclers looked with suspicion on these packs of teenagers, who loudly sang their pilgrimage songs, because they were beyond all social control, hence sinister and dangerous. Niklashausen also attracted many teenagers.

The town chronicler of Erfurt has left us a penetrating and sympathetic account of the pilgrimage to Wilsnack in 1475, in which most of the pilgrims were "children." During the previous year (1474), he said, the harvests had been bad, and many child-pilgrims had come from poor homes:

... for the days are very long and empty of things to do and many are driven to pilgrimage for lack of bread to eat. ... Having no bread, and being too poor to stay with friends or neighbors, they were ashamed to go begging near their own homes. And so they decided to go on a pilgrimage and beg in each town on the route, reckoning that it was better to beg in a strange district than from people they knew. And that is why there were so many young boys among them. ... When curious onlookers asked them why they did it, they sought to explain themselves by saying they were driven by an irresistible impulse.

The tens of thousands of peasant pilgrims who went to Niklashausen a year later in 1476, no doubt, were driven by a variety of reasons. A pilgrimage was enchanted time and space that combined the rowdiness of Carnival with the self-denial of Lent, and it drew both rowdy and ascetic people into its vortex. The pious came in troops with their banners and great candles before them. The poor came seeking alms to keep alive. The oppressed came to express grievances over taxes and tolls and to level society to one rank. And there were the con men, who cynically preyed on the gullible by faking miracles. Others came for adventure or simply to get out of their tight little villages. Gangs of young men were there to tweak the noses of the authorities. They all came to Niklashausen as if in a crazydance-frenzy of the plague years: hand in hand, saint and sinner, young and old, sane and loony, all danced to the music of their young prophet, Hans Behem, the Drummer of Niklashausen.

In the late 1540s, more than seventy years after the events in Niklashausen had taken place, Georg Widman included in his *Chronika* a long section on the Drummer of Niklashausen. This is the type of information that survived in clerical circles over the generations, and on which we must rely for descriptions of the pilgrimage. Widman's contempt for the Drummer and for the ignorance of common folk is obvious:

All Germany seemed to be in commotion. . . . So great was the crush that the drummer, who was then staying in a farmhouse, stuck his head out of a window in the roof so that the crowd might see him and hear him preach. And some say that a Franciscan monk was seen standing at his back, prompting him as he spoke. When his sermon had ended, the pilgrims began to bewail their sins, though it may be that it was really the drink in them causing their misery. They cut the long points off their shoes (pointed shoes being then in fashion) and trimmed their hair, and it seemed as though a dozen carts would not suffice to haul away the hair and shoes being discarded that day, to say nothing of embroidered kerchiefs, robes, doublets, and other female and male adornments. Many men and women took off all their clothes and left them in the church [of Niklashausen], going away naked except for their shifts. Before they had traveled a mile from Niklashausen, however, with the noise and the wine abating in their heads, they began to regret having abandoned their clothing. And an incredible amount of money was donated by these pilgrims, also wax and wax candles stuck like hedgehogs with coins of neighboring cities and regions.

The drummer wore on his head a kind of cap with tufts on it. A few among the people who could reach him tore these tufts from his cap, believing them to have the power to cure ills and ease pain. Women in labor swore that application of one of these tufts to the belly guaranteed a safe delivery. Wherever the drummer went, people touched his hands and his staff, thinking these to be capable of wonderful cures.

Widman had to rely in part on earlier chroniclers for his information. One major version of the affair that Widman drew from was written in 1514 by Johann Trithemius, then an old man and abbot of a Benedictine monastery in Würzburg. Trithemius probably had access to the archives of the bishop of Würzburg as well as to the memories (and fantasies) of witnesses. His account clearly was influenced by Sebastian Brant's best-seller, *The Ship of Fools* (1494), in which the Drummer (or Piper, as Brant called him) of Niklashausen was given a chapter to himself: the Piper and his followers, said Brant, were fools for their disdain for the Holy Scriptures; the foolish people listened to the foolish visions of the fool Piper. Fools and their novelties fit the Niklashausen pilgrimage perfectly for Trithemius, who lauded *The Ship of Fools* as "a most agreeable and salubrious book" and called it the "Divine Satire" to complement Dante's "Divine Comedy." Trithemius' historical narrative, built around the theme of fools, then became "historical reality" for many historians, such as Georg Widman, thereafter.

In the aforesaid year [1476] in East Franconia in the diocese of Würzburg there took place a gathering of the people from all over Germany to see a certain man by the name of Hans of Niklashausen, a peasant, an extremely ignorant half-wit, and herdsman of pigs. It was a great and astonishing thing, the likes of which had never been seen before. I do not know whether he was led astray by an evil spirit or perhaps by insanity, but he publicly preached certain novelties—with simpleness and foolishness—in fields and meadows and even from the window of some peasant's small hut or from trees. Since he was neither able to speak well nor able to propose anything that could be comprehended, a certain man of the mendicant friars, in concealment, whispered instructions to him on what he should preach. Thus, often he would speak from a high window to the crowd below so that he could have his teacher in hiding at his ear. But in fact it was apparent that the friar was whispering to him.

So many people came daily in troops to hear this pitiable little fool that it has been recorded that often in one day there were ten thousand people, on another day twenty thousand, and even sometimes thirty thousand people converged on the village of Niklashausen to hear him. People came not only from eastern Franconia but also from Bavaria and Swabia, from Alsace and places along the Rhine, from Wittemberg, from Hesse, from Thuringia and Saxony. He preached newfangled beliefs against the clergy and princes which he imagined had been revealed to him visibly and sensibly by the Most Blessed Virgin Mary in a field where he was herding pigs. Because of that, simple people honored and venerated him as a holy man; they elevated him as a prophet of God and a teacher of truth of the divine faith—all because the Mother of God should have deemed him worthy of gentle conversation before all mankind.

Thus, just as we have heard from those who were actually present, such a great multitude of people used to gather around him daily that sometimes he was in danger of being crushed as people eagerly rushed to see him. And often, he had great difficulty finding the time or place to satisfy nature in order to eat, drink, relieve his bowels, or sleep. The masses who gathered about him sought with fervent desire to see and touch and talk to the holy man of God. He who was able to touch the holy man, or even his garments, reckoned himself sanctified and blessed. In such great foolishness, the multitude of ignorant people pushed forward. With overwhelming desire, they all wanted to have any little piece of his cloak, because they believed that it had been sanctified as if it were a relic of a saint. They cut with knives and pulled off with their hands pieces of the little fool's clothing, just as often as anybody was allowed to approach him. Thus, they constantly tore away from him whatever they were able to grab so that the pitiful wretch was stripped almost daily and was compelled to find new cloaks from the piles of oblations of those pilgrims who had left them at the church.

The masses of stupid people followed the fool everywhere. Along his path, in a procession, they kneeled down before him, and then clasping their hands together said, "Pray for me to God, holy man." With his hand he then quickly made the sign of the cross—rather than praying. So great was the joy of the person to whom he made a sign of benediction that he believed himself actually to be blessed and that all his sins were absolved before God. The rush of people running to meet him was continuous, not only during the day, but also at night. . . . There was great security for the people who walked in such great numbers, because they marched in troops or squadrons, and during the nighttime hours they slept in meadows or fields or in the woods, and no one feared danger of any sort.

People imagined that many miracles took place either in the chapel of Niklashausen or before the little fool, Hänsel. No miracle in truth happened, but rather all were fabricated, false, and feigned. Oblations in gold, silver, jewels, money, wax, and great heaps of clothing were given by the pilgrims. They strove hard to do their foolish devotions—which clearly were neither to the honor of God nor of any use whatsoever to the Church.

Why was the distinguished old Abbot Johann Trithemius, a historian and scholar, so mean-spirited about the Drummer almost forty years after the pilgrimage? It was not just that he drew his theme from Sebastian Brant. He made Hans into a herder of *pigs,* which nobody before him had done. The Drummer's association with swine carried all of its modern derogatory associations—rather than with sheep, which recalled the holy shepherds of the Nativity. In an earlier, shorter account in 1506, he merely called the Drummer a pastor of brute animals. Trithemius was also one of the first chroniclers to suggest that the Drummer was coached in his preaching by a concealed mendicant friar; contemporary witnesses gave only ambiguous indications of the presence of a Dominican friar at Niklashausen, but not as Hans' coach.

Was the abbot merely angry about Hans' blasphemy in claiming a vision? No. There was no reason why the Virgin should not appear to shepherds. Rather, what was so offensive was what the Virgin supposedly told Hans to say. She told him to preach against the sins of the clergy and that the peasant-pilgrims should not pay their rents or tithes to them. Moreover, the Virgin told him, "Say to all the people that my son wishes and orders that all tolls, levies, forced labor, exactions, payments and aids required of the prelates, princes, and nobles be abolished completely and at once. They shall oppress the poor no more." Finally, the Drummer received a divine revelation that the woods and the waters of the earth should be held in common for the use and pleasure of all the faithful in Christ and not for just the rich. This was a pilgrimage message of "leveling" of society. For the old abbot, it was crazy, perhaps just like Carnival, "as if the poor were wealthy and a peasant were a bishop or a prince." He continues in bitterness:

> So, great multitudes of rustic, ignorant people gathered together daily in Niklashausen. They discussed and talked of nothing except how they could accomplish what Hänsel instructed them to do, as if the instructions had been brought forth from the mouth of God. Indeed, what could peasants find more agreeable than that they had been freed from all payment of rents and tenant services, and that thereafter they would hold everything in common with the clergy and princes? Truly, what could a layman find more desirable than that he should see the clergy and priests immediately stripped of all privileges and liberties, and denied their collection of tithes, rents, and the proceeds of the holy altar? So, the little fool stirred up laymen and laywomen to come from all over Germany to Niklashausen. The people seemed to be directed there only by the sermons of this little idiot and his claim that peasants would become free and the clergy placed in servitude.

# V

# The Feast of Corpus Christi

In the eyes of the authorities, the Drummer was a dangerous player of foolish music, leading his followers in a crazy, egalitarian dance that promised only social chaos. He had to be stopped, so wrote Archbishop Dieter to Bishop Rudolph on June 13, and his perilous doctrines rooted out of popular belief.

Thursday, June 13, was the Feast of Corpus Christi, one of the major festival days of medieval Europe—and an especially appropriate day for the assertion of hierarchical authority against the Carnival-Lent-Crazy Dance-Pilgrimage of the Drummer of Niklashausen.

The Feast of Corpus Christi had originated with an Augustinian nun named Juliana of Liège, who in 1209 had a vision of a bright, full moon, marred only by a small, dark spot. She interpreted the moon to represent the church and the dark spot to represent the absence of a separate feast in honor of the Eucharist. Juliana belonged to a generation that was especially sensitive to the sacrament of the Eucharist and the arguments over transubstantiation, that is, that the sacramental host becomes the body of Christ *(corpus Christi)*. Her cause for a new feast day to celebrate the Eucharist was taken up by the archdeacon of Liège, Jacques Pantaléon. In 1246, the feast of the Eucharist (or Corpus Christi) was made a feast day in the diocese of Liège, celebrated on the Thursday after the octave (eighth day) of Pentecost. When Archdeacon Jacques became Pope Urban IV, he made the local feast of Liège a feast for the entire church.

During the fourteenth and fifteenth centuries throughout Europe, the Feast of Corpus Christi was noted for a great procession of townsfolk who carried the Eucharist through their streets and into the countryside. Everybody participated in the procession, from the highest in rank and status to the lowest. If we were to ask participants what was going on, they would probably say that they and their fellow citizens were celebrating the triumph of Christ the King.

As outsiders we may see it as a celebration of the triumph of hierarchy, wealth, and rank. For this is what was on parade and reinforced in everybody's mind: the social hierarchy and the relative ranking of everybody in a community. The Corpus Christi procession forced the elite of a town such as Würzburg to rank everybody in society and put them physically in their place—which was just the opposite of Carnival, just the opposite of the egalitarian pilgrimage that had formed outside the walls of Würzburg. Thus, we may also see the display of power of the bishop and townsmen of Würzburg on the Feast of Corpus Christi as an inverted mirror image, or a counterpoint, to the Drummer and his pilgrims.

So, on June 13, Corpus Christi Day, the day that Bishop Rudolph was given full authority to stop the Drummer, the bishop marched in a procession of power, authority, and hierarchy. First came the mendicant friars, followed by monastic clergy, both as escorts to the secular clergy, who were led by the bishop, who in turn carried a vessel containing the Eucharist, or the body of Christ. Then came the town council, the masters of the crafts, and so on, down to the servants of the burghers. Nobody doubted that Bishop Rudolph was the most powerful man in Würzburg and its surrounding countryside.

Against Bishop Rudolph and lords like him stood the peasant pilgrims in Niklashausen. Each side saw the other as a dark spot on their full moon of true piety.

Würzburg was one of those quintessential German creations: a prince-bishopric, or a lordship of a city under the secular as well as the ecclesiastical control of a bishop. Germany, especially in the south and along the Rhine, was dotted with them, and each had its own unique history. Each one, however, emerged from a struggle among the bishop, his cathedral chapter (which was relatively independent and often at odds with the bishop), and the leading townsmen for control of the town (and consequently of the countryside).

In Würzburg, the struggle for control of the city was settled by 1400 with the complete triumph of the bishop, who was granted by townsmen the power to levy and collect city taxes as well as the right to appoint the mayor to head the town council. The town council of Würzburg had lost all power and political meaning. Members of the council after 1444 were also appointed by the bishop and the cathedral chapter and became mere functionaries in the bishop's administration.

During the fifteenth century, the bishops of Würzburg followed the pattern of other German princes to establish independent territorial states. This was expensive and often involved them in border wars with neighboring princes—especially in Franconia, which, even by German standards, was unusually fragmented among territorial lords. Bishops employed expensive gangs of knights for internal security, and had to pay for elaborate (and expensive) displays of ceremonial power.

Money was a constant concern for the bishops of Würzburg—as well as for all other state-building princes. The bishops had to exploit all sources of potential income to pay the enormous cathedral debts that had built up since the late fourteenth century through mismanagement of lands and from the economic forces that had turned against landlords. Most of the bishop's lands were heavily mortgaged and brought in no revenue at all, only bills. Hence, the bishops taxed their subjects relentlessly during the fifteenth century. There were always new market tolls that merchants had to pay—and passed on to their buyers. River tolls were imposed on those crossing the Main River, either to enter Würzburg or to leave it to go south. Bishops fully exploited their taxing powers just to stay financially even.

Throughout the entire fifteenth century, townsmen complained constantly to the bishops about taxes. But to no avail. The bishop and the cathedral answered evasion of taxes and tolls with prosecution in their ecclesiastical courts.

By the 1470s the prince-bishopric of Würzburg was financially solvent—barely—through the tough management of a few financially responsible bishops and through ruthlessly efficient collection of taxes, tolls, and duties.

Collection from whom? Not the clergy. By special rights and privileges accorded them as clergy, they were completely free from all principal taxes and duties. These privileges of exemption extended even to the secular vassals and selected servants of the clergy. This, of course, was odious to townsfolk and laymen throughout the diocese. Privileges were all so visible and open: a priest crossed the bridge at Würzburg freely and a layman had to dig into his purse to pay the toll.

Clearly, the clergy were set apart from others by their privileges. Even if they committed a crime, they did not have to face a secular court or secular laws. Rather, they were tried in a church court—by other clergy. This was known as "benefit of clergy."

The clergy were also set apart by their monopoly on dispensing God's "grace" through the mass. They were set apart financially as privileged receivers of wealth, not producers. They were set apart socially by their education and their specific dress. At every turn in Würzburg—and often elsewhere—they were encased in "privilege" in its original meaning of "private law."

So who paid the bishop's debts? Laymen: townsmen and peasants principally.

Würzburg may be seen as Everytown. It differed from other cities and principalities in Germany only in details, not in primary forms: everywhere in fifteenth-century Germany we find the same state building by local princes; increased taxes, duties, and tolls; a privileged clergy or nobility, or both, living off the "tribute" (taxes, and so forth) of an embattled, subject peasantry; anticlericalism; pilgrimages and processions.

Hence, many people were willing to listen to preachers who thundered against the wealth and power of the official church. A fifteenth-century Beghard preacher, Hermann Kuchner, drew large, enthusiastic crowds in Würzburg diocese when he called for the poverty of the church, and when he preached against the doctrines of hell and purgatory, calling them inventions of the clergy. He addressed directly the material and spiritual salvation of lay folk. Also during the fifteenth century, many Hussite refugees and preachers passed through Franconia from Bohemia—only fifty or so miles east of the Tauber Valley—preaching against the clergy and purgatory.

Anticlerical ideas and sermons were not new to southern Germany. The tens of thousands of people who went to Niklashausen to hear the Drummer preach against the clergy and their property merely demonstrated yet once again the deep and widespread resentment of clerical wealth and privilege that had been voiced many times earlier. In 1476, the message was the same; only the cast of players had changed. Now the Drummer railed against Bishop Rudolph and his clergy.

It is tempting to see Hans the Drummer and Bishop Rudolph as opposites in the drama of Niklashausen: as youth against age (Rudolph was seventy-five years old in 1476); as innocent virtue against bureaucratic villainy; as the voice of the oppressed against the voice of the oppressor. To a certain extent this was true: the clergy of the diocese of Würzburg were the oppressors through their privileges; and peasants worked and paid, worked and paid. But Bishop Rudolph does not fit our clichés about an unprincipled, grasping, evil, villainous, medieval bishop; and, ironically, he and the Drummer shared much the same reforming zeal.

To understand why most of the local population of Würzburg remained loyal to the bishop in 1476—while others danced to the Drummer's anticlerical tune—we must look briefly at the history of Bishop Rudolph's predecessors and at the problem of "reform" in the fifteenth-century church.

When church leaders spoke of "reform" and "reformation" of the church in the fifteenth century, they generally meant the reform of the clergy by a higher authority, that is, a bishop, archbishop, or church council. And by "reform" they meant literally to re-form the clergy, that is, church leaders were to "form them again" into an earlier mold of the primitive church. To reform meant to look back to a Golden Age, a morally pure time when Christian men and women were truly virtuous. This was pure romanticism, of course, and assumed that men and women—notably the clergy—behaved better during some misty past age than in the present. It also meant that present-day clergy necessarily fell short of the ideal past. Reformers in the official church continually harped on the shortcomings of the workaday clergy.

Articulate lay people outside the official church also criticized the clergy incessantly and looked back to an earlier, purer model of behavior. Beghards, Hussites, and other lay preachers called for the poverty of the church, just as the "reforming" wing of the Franciscans, the Observants, had preached the ideal of apostolic poverty. This was *their* idea of "reform," to re-form the entire church into the mold of poverty of the apostolic age.

In the everyday world of church administration, bishops generally were content merely to reform clerical dress and behavior by reinforcing the lines of authority between bishop and priest. Apostolic poverty was not the issue. Discipline was. And discipline, said the reformers, was best done through a bureaucracy whereby a church council issues orders and codes of behavior, which are then reissued and enforced by reform-minded bishops down to the parish level.

The goals of reformers often had less to do with the well-being of the laity than with removing the causes of ridicule and abuse of the clergy by lay folk. Bishops must put their houses in order; lines of authority must be established; anticlericalism must be squelched; and power must be returned to local bishops and archbishops through the recovery of their economic power.

The history of the men who became bishops of Würzburg during the fifteenth century explains much about their failure to reform an entrenched clergy, and about their slight influence on the religious sensibilities of common folk. Our story of the Würzburg bishops properly begins with the long rule of Johann von Brun from 1411 to 1440. These were the years of the great, reforming church councils of Constance (1414–1418) and Basel (1431–1449). But Bishop Johann von Brun was no reformer. Rather, he lived the extravagant, profligate life of a great prince, lavishing vast sums of money on pomp and displays of power. Bishop Johann drove the diocese deeply into debt, and irresponsibly mortgaged diocesan property, offices, and rights. To make ends meet, he exploited his economic privileges over the laity through crushing taxation.

The diocese took a dramatic turn in 1443 when a canon of the cathedral, Gottfried Shenk von Limpurg, was elected bishop with the strong support of the new emperor, Frederick III. Von Limpurg was a full-blown reformer, straight out of the ideal mold of the reforming councils. For his relatively brief reign until 1455, von Limpurg brought austerity to diocesan finances to pay its huge debts. By the early 1450s expenditures were finally reduced to where they equaled income.

Austerity, of course, meant more than mere careful living. It also meant collecting all that was due the bishop in tolls and taxes. Von Limpurg was widely respected in clerical and political circles as an honest, reforming bishop, but his reign seems to have made little impact on the lives of common folk who were still gouged at every turn by a privileged clergy. Reform did little for their material salvation.

Von Limpurg did not stop at financial reform, however. He tried to enforce discipline on his clergy. In regularly called synods, he issued codes for their behavior and dress: sleeves should be narrowly cut without fashionable slits; shoes should not have fancy long points; clergy were not to participate in jousts and tourneys, or to dance in taverns; and they were not—under strong threats—to have concubines, who usually were disguised as cooks and servants.

This was the common stuff of all clerical reform movements, and largely ineffective. Later bishops had to issue the same injunctions time and again. Nevertheless, periodic self-examinations by the clergy tended to call attention to their shortcomings. High church officials were saying publicly that the clergy *were* in need of reform and correction. Von Limpurg did not challenge the privileges of the clergy, but said they abused their privileged place in society by their vanities and immorality. He justified privilege by the clean living of a worthy clergy.

Von Limpurg in his reforms had responded not only to the cries for "reformation" coming from church councils but also to the more immediate anticlericalism of wandering preachers, who were often heretical, often Hussite. He had to answer such men as Friedrich Müller, who in 1446, like a tornado, cut a swath through central Germany with his Hussite preaching against clerical wealth and privilege, and against purgatory, which, he said, had been concocted by the clergy. Müller appealed directly to the material and spiritual salvation of common folk and drew enormous, enthusiastic crowds wherever he went. After the dust had settled, hundreds of men and women throughout Germany, including 127 in Würzburg alone, were forced to abjure the heretical opinions that they had picked up from Müller and to perform public penance. Bishops such as von Limpurg knew that because people abjured their heresies they did not stop believing them. Von Limpurg's strategy for eradicating heretical ideas—ideas founded on a deeply cynical anticlericalism—was to remove the cause of complaints against the clergy. But he was able with only marginal success to turn his priests into pastors of their flocks rather than wolves who devoured them.

At von Limpurg's death in 1455, the cathedral chapter—which had opposed the reforming bishop at every turn—elected one of their own and the leader of the opposition to von Limpurg: Johann von Grumbach. They could not have made a worse choice. The chapter soon lived to regret the election of this crabby, quarrelsome man. He was the prototype of the careerist churchman: indifferent to his spiritual functions, obsessed with his position among other German princes, disdainful of underlings. For his entire rule until 1466, he feuded and warred against his princely neighbors.

Wars and arming for wars demanded increased income, and the central question of von Grumbach's reign was how to raise more, and yet more, money. Again the bishop of Würzburg mortgaged his properties and his rights (for example, the granting of appointments to lesser offices). He squeezed every possible penny from town and country in taxes, tolls, duties, and labor services. Oppressive, bloodsucking tribute taking was the order of the day. The diocese of Würzburg systematically was turned into a region of financial devastation.

Those who fared well despite the exploitive rule of von Grumbach were, of course, the clergy whose privileges exempted them from all major taxes and tolls. Laymen and laywomen listened with enthusiasm to powerful, dynamic preachers such as John of Capistrano, who called for the poverty of the clergy, and to less orthodox preachers who hammered home the same message. In 1458, Friedrich Reiser, the leader of the German Waldensians, passed through Würzburg on his preaching trip across Germany and drew enormous, sympathetic crowds in his call for clerical poverty. Other lay preachers wandered the countryside in imitation of the apostles, calling for the holy poverty of the church. Against the traveling preachers were the entrenched, privileged clergy of Würzburg—and of other dioceses throughout Germany—who looked especially rapacious in comparison.

When von Grumbach died in 1466, the lay population of the prince-bishopric of Würzburg was impoverished from ruthless taxation, and the land was devastated by armies and bandits who had been unleashed in von Grumbach's wars and feuds. The bishop's own treasury was empty, his properties mortgaged, and payments on his many notes were due. When he died, no one shed a tear for him. Throughout Franconia were heard folksongs that portrayed von Grumbach and his henchmen burning in hell.

Whom should the chapter now elect? They chose what for them perhaps was a compromise candidate, a man already sixty-five years old, hence too old, they perhaps thought, to rock the boat or to do much damage. If they thought thus, then they badly misjudged this little old man, Rudolph von Sherenberg, who proved to be a vigorous reforming bishop until his death in 1495 at the age of ninety-four. Rudolph had been the cathedral teacher *(Domscholaster)* and a high administrator under von Grumbach, that is, he was part of the old administration yet trusted by the cathedral chapter. He was also a reformer in the mold of Gottfried von Limpurg.

Bishop Rudolph's plan for reform in his diocese was simple and sound. He realized that power—control over people—was at bottom economic. When the bishop's properties and rights were mortgaged away, so were his power and influence. If he mortgaged an estate with the accompanying right to appoint the local parish priest, he lost control over the character and behavior of that priest. Loss of income equaled loss of influence. The previous bishop, Johann von Grumbach, had mortgaged virtually everything, which left Bishop Rudolph in a dire position. He could not reform the clergy without economic control over their appointments.

Thus Rudolph's first task was to redeem the debts of the diocese, that is, to repurchase his rights and properties. Again, the bishop's household practiced austerity in order to increase income. Year by year he redeemed his debts and mortgages.

Bishop Rudolph's second aim in his reform was to pacify the land. He smoothed over old feuds and the bitter feelings of neighboring princes with conciliatory gestures. No more feuds. No more war.

His third goal was to regulate the lives of the clergy. Their reform must begin with their education. The older, entrenched clergy may not be able to be reached through education, but the younger ones could. But how? Würzburg did not have an intellectual culture. It was not yet a university town. If it had a printing press, however, then the bishop could disseminate knowledge without end, and so Bishop Rudolph gave the city its first printing press, to publish the books and pamphlets needed for his religious reform program. He succeeded in placing devotional and liturgical books into the hands of all his clergy, down to the lowliest village priest. Books of sermons were published as well as devotional books for literate laity. The Würzburg printing press was famous throughout Germany for its liturgical and devotional books.

Bishop Rudolph was determined to make his clergy a model of the Christian life in their behavior and dress. His model was essentially the same as the Drummer's and the heretical preachers and the fire-breathing Observant Franciscans: simplicity without the vanities of fashion. Like John of Capistrano and the Drummer of Niklashausen, Bishop Rudolph spoke out—and issued injunctions—against slit doublets and pointed shoes. These were vanities that called attention to oneself rather than to one's religious calling. Especially those pointed shoes.

Reformers such as Rudolph were often a grim bunch. Their zeal for right living slipped easily into sanctimony and pomposity. Is it any wonder that such gloomy seriousness was greeted with an explosion of laughter and ridicule at Carnival? But, alas, reform is high-minded, serious business that requires earnest, sober people to enforce earnest, sober behavior—whether the reformer be a medieval bishop or a Victorian temperance leader or a modern professorial Keeper of Academic Piety. That damned, crude, mocking laughter always escapes from the lower ranks. For Bishop Rudolph, the streets of Würzburg had to be cleared of noisy, disreputable characters. He was especially troubled by the singing in the streets, the dancing, the revelry, the wild Carnival atmosphere that so often rocked Würzburg on feast and market days. The old reformer, like reformers before and after him, tried to control people's laughter, that maniacal hilarity that made bishops, mayors, and princes the butt of jokes, and thus conquered lower-class fear of authority. He issued several injunctions against people singing and dancing in the streets, not just because they were a public annoyance, but because they were not sober, earnest Christians: dancing was the means by which the devil possessed people; they lost their reason and gave themselves over to movements of self-indulgent joy.

Thus the social function of reform was to compel powerful men of the elite to define and categorize people according to a standard of the Good Christian: sober, earnest, and pious. Outside the standard was the Bad Christian (sinner), the Anti-Christian (heretic and witch), and the Non-Christian (Jew), all of whom became increasingly and more sharply defined to the reforming generations of the late fifteenth century. Heretics were generally left alone in Germany during the late fifteenth century, but such was not the case for witches and Jews. Witches, we all now know, came to be defined in the late fifteenth century as consorts of the devil rather than as mere magicians. They were primarily an invention of intellectuals, notably two German Dominican Inquisitors: Heinrich Kramer (the Inquisitor for southern Germany) and Jacob Sprenger (the Inquisitor for the Rhineland). Jews also became a "problem" for German reformers, and had to be redefined in legal terms. Reformers confronted Jewish communities everywhere in Germany—unlike in England or in France, which had long since expelled its Jews.

Anti-Semitic outbursts were common in fifteenth-century Germany. And we would expect to find in Niklashausen in 1476, during great religious frenzy, vicious undertones of anti-Semitism. But it was scarcely present. The absence of anti-Semitism at Niklashausen is astonishing and begs for an explanation.

The "Jewish problem" had occupied most of the reign of Bishop Rudolph. He, like every other bishop, had to face the Jewish community, to confront Jewish wealth, their lending, their protection by the princes of Germany. Princes defended Jews and gave them special, protected standing, because they were a rich reservoir of wealth that could be tapped at will through taxes or threats. Debt-ridden bishops, like von Grumbach, also protected the Jewish community for the same reason: he needed their wealth. A reforming bishop such as Rudolph, however, could not stand idly by and allow Jews a privileged position in Christian society, the "body of Christ." They were a cancer, and the reformer, as doctor, must remove the disease. These were the anthropomorphic metaphors that governed social thought in the fifteenth century and which compelled serious, responsible men to define whole groups of people out of society.

During the middle years of the fifteenth century, the legal and social position of Jewish families in the diocese of Würzburg had grown stronger: in part because of the moderate legislation of the church by Cardinal Nicholas of Cusa during the 1450s that gave Jews a legal position in Christian society; in part because of Bishop von Grumbach's incessant need for money, which led him to grant favorable treatment to his Jewish lenders. Thus Rudolph upon becoming bishop in 1466 was faced with a "Jewish problem," not only because Jews were living in relative peace in the body of Christ, but also because he saw their financial power as harmful to his flock. He held Jewish money lenders responsible for the pauperization of the countryside, for the debts at high interest rates that ground down his peasants. He said much less about the profligate mismanagement of the previous prince-bishops of Würzburg. One of his obsessions was to regulate usury in the Jewish quarters of his diocese: debts of all Christians to Jews must be redeemed.

In 1475, just one year before the pilgrimage to Niklashausen, a wave of ugly anti-Semitism swept over Germany. It began in the emperor's city of Trent in northern Italy following the murder of a young Christian boy. Popular sentiment immediately blamed the Jews by appealing to the old shibboleth that Jews ritually murdered little Christian boys. News of the crime spread through Germany during 1475 and 1476, leaving in its wake many pogroms against Jewish communities. Bishop Rudolph was easily caught up in the anti-

Semitic hysteria and ordered the expulsion of all Jews from the diocese of Würzburg. But he never carried out his own order. When the hysteria died down, Jews were still in the diocese and little had changed.

At the time of the pilgrimage to Niklashausen, anti-Semitism should have been vocal and explosive as it was throughout Germany. We should expect in the Drummer's railing against financial oppression and gouging, in his cry for the leveling of all social ranks and for all goods to be held in common, that he would include Jewish money lenders in his outrage. But we hear nothing of the sort, not from the Drummer, not from his tens of thousands of followers. Yet, the atmosphere was right. As was the cause of the poor.

What the silence suggests is that the "Jewish problem" that fills fifteenth-century diocesan archives was more a problem of authorities—like witchcraft—than it was of common people. It also suggests that the many debts of peasants in the countryside were not to Jews, but to landlords in the form of sharecropping as credit. Perhaps only the elite used Jewish moneylenders for credit. This is an argument from the silence of the records, of course, but the silence, especially in 1476, is startling. For the peasant-pilgrims, the enemy was the elite of Christian society, not Jewish moneylenders, who also were victims of Christian authorities.

By early June 1476, after more than a month of watching hordes of people troop past Würzburg to Niklashausen, the authorities in Würzburg became understandably nervous. There were more people on the roads outside the city walls than made up the entire population of the town, which numbered only about five thousand. The pilgrims were all freed from normal social constraints, and many sang dangerous-sounding pilgrimage songs in which new words against the clergy had been added to old familiar tunes.

On Tuesday, June 18, the scribe of the town council reported in his minutes that a certain Burckart Metzler had heard alarming murmuring among the pilgrims that they would *kill all the priests*. If the report was correct, then the strange pilgrimage to Niklashausen was turning into the authorities' worst nightmare: a popular uprising driven by religious fantasies of the destruction of the social hierarchy. The council sent for Burckart Metzler to hear from his own mouth what was happening outside the town walls.

In the meantime, the town quartermaster and master of accounts were ordered to ensure adequate supplies of food, water, and munitions in the event of violence from the pilgrims. The council also resolved that the pilgrims be exempted from paying the bridge toll across the Main River. Yes, there was great concern for the loss of toll revenues and the necessity of new taxes to maintain the bridge, but it was more important to allow easy passage of the mobs of pilgrims *away* from Würzburg. The records do not state this, but the council must have recognized the obvious danger and folly of trying to stop thousands of people at the gates of Würzburg . . . and then demanding money from them. Better to let them go on their way.

On the next day, June 19, all the powerful men in Würzburg gathered in the cathedral chapterhouse to discuss the Niklashausen affair. Here was Bishop Rudolph himself, with representatives of the cathedral chapter, the mayor, and the town council. They again issued urgent orders to the quartermaster and the master of accounts to ensure food and water supplies; shortages could easily touch off food riots *within* the city. All residents were ordered to have adequate buckets and bottles of water by their front doors in case of fire.

Burckart Metzler appeared before this extraordinary assembly, along with his companion, one Kempffennagel. It must have been a frustrating experience for the authorities, because neither man was able to say anything about the rumors of impending violence. Both gave rambling accounts of their activities to collect money to buy candles, banners, and painted standards for the pilgrims to carry to Niklashausen. The pilgrimage through their eyes seemed so innocent.

—Tell us, Metzler, what exactly were you doing among the pilgrims?

—I sought out wives and maidens for contributions to buy candles to offer the Virgin in Niklashausen. I told them that if they would give up only two meals, then the money saved would buy two candles.

Don't get me wrong. I didn't enter any woman's house. I know what you are thinking. No. I begged for money on the roads and pathways, and collected the money in a hat. If I have done anything wrong I beg your forgiveness. I know nothing else.

—And you, Kempffennagel, what do you know?

—My wife is a candlemaker, and some maidens and wives came to her and asked her to make two candles. The women used a portion of their money to buy a banner for the pilgrimage. So they bought a pole and a crosspiece on which to hang a standard. They then hired a painter to paint two large keys crossing. I know nothing else.

Candles? Candles? What is all this about candles? And a standard with crossed keys? What about the murder of priests? The bishop and the others wanted to hear about the impending violence, not about candlemaking and perfectly orthodox banners with crossed keys (that is, the common heraldic symbol of papal power).


Dangerous events, in fact, were taking place outside the walls of Würzburg. The Drummer was preaching and pilgrims were singing his revolutionary songs.


The end of June marked the great Midsummer's Eve celebration of June 23, before the feast of St. John the Baptist (June 24). This again was a great peasant festival that signaled the end of the sacred half of the year which had begun with Advent. Midsummer was an old pagan festival that celebrated the summer solstice, but which now had a Christian veneer associated with a saint's day. An early sixteenth-century source tells us that in almost every village and town in Germany, great bonfires were lit on Midsummer's Eve and people of all ages, male and female, gathered about the bonfires to sing and dance. Midsummer was a fleeting, enchanted, liminal time.

Another medieval source tells us that boys burned bones and other filth to make a foul smoke which was supposed to drive away dragons who copulated in the warm summer air. The dragons also poisoned wells and rivers. Throughout Germany, so says our witness, Midsummer's Eve is marked by three things: a great bonfire, a procession of peasants with their torches around their fields, and a great burning wheel that young men roll down a nearby hill. Our source tells us that the wheel symbolizes the sun, which now at its highest point in the sky begins its descent to winter.

In the town of Würzburg, the bishop's servants gathered at the Frauenberg (Our Lady's Mount) at the bishop's castle, which overlooked the city, and using flexible sticks they threw burning disks of wood from the castle walls. The darkness gave them the appearance of fiery dragons. In the towns around Würzburg, people wore garlands of mugwort and vervain on their heads, and looked at the fire through bunches of larkspur in the belief that it would improve their eyesight. As they departed, they threw their mugwort and vervain into the fire and said, "May all my ill luck depart and be burnt up with these."

Sometime during the final days of June, after Midsummer, the town councils of both Würzburg and Mainz—the two great prince-bishoprics—met together at Aschaffenburg to devise a strategy to stop "the Drummer, called Hans Behem" *(der peucker, Johann Beham genannt)*. They wanted him imprisoned, interrogated, and his teachings condemned. But thus far they only had secondhand reports of what was happening in Niklashausen. If they were to rid themselves of the Drummer, they wanted to do it legally. But to act legally or otherwise against him would be difficult, because at that moment tens of thousands of people were either in Niklashausen or on their way to hear the Drummer give an eagerly awaited sermon on the Feast of the Visitation of Mary, Tuesday, July 2—just a few days away.

The authorities agreed on several resolutions. If the Drummer could not be seized during the coming week—they obviously saw real problems in arresting him—then an order of excommunication against him was to be issued to all parishes in the two dioceses. All subjects of Mainz and Würzburg were forbidden, also under pain of excommunication, from having anything to do with the Drummer. They could not meet him, eat or drink with him, listen to him preach, or believe anything he said. It was forbidden for any of his teachings to be publicly preached in either diocese. (The writer left this sentence in the vague, passive voice to include anybody and everybody.) And no one was to preach without a license from one of the bishops. Apparently masses were being celebrated at portable altars—by whom we do not know—because portable altars were also banned from the entire Tauber Valley.

The authorities needed a notarized eyewitness account of the Drummer's preaching in order to make a legal case against him. What better opportunity to have the Drummer convict himself with his own words than to witness and record his crucial sermon on July 2, the Feast of the Visitation of Mary? Therefore they ordered that "witnesses"—two or more notarized witnesses were needed to convict the Drummer at his anticipated trial—go to Niklashausen to hear Hans, but "in a secret and careful manner" (in einer geheime und versorglich geschee). The spies were to write down anything damaging that could be used against Hans.

The authorities were closing in on the Drummer.

In the minutes of this extraordinary meeting, we get our first indication that Hans may have been helped by a mendicant friar. The authorities had heard rumors of a Dominican friar (einen prediger monch) who was also preaching at Niklashausen. We do not, and perhaps cannot, know what this friar was doing. Did he coach the Drummer? Was he a renegade friar who took advantage of an extraordinary situation? Was he even a Dominican? Perhaps they confused the "friar" with the strange Beghard hermit who we know was at Niklashausen.

The authorities no doubt were fuzzy in their grasp of what was actually happening at Niklashausen. However, they were much more certain of the dangerous power of the songs of the pilgrims, some of which had been composed by the Drummer. They expressly forbade anyone, again under pain of excommunication, from singing any of the songs or rhymes composed by the Drummer. As in any revolutionary movement and moment, the songs must have been highly inflammatory, with the now-serious mocking tone of Carnival. They would have served to bind the many strangers at Niklashausen together in a common cause. Unfortunately the Drummer's songs have not survived, but we do have two verses that authorities vividly remembered. They were probably sung to the tune of a common pilgrimage song, and they are based on the well-known opening litany, between priest and congregation, of the mass:

> Oh God in Heaven, on you we call,
>     Kyrie Eleison.
> Help us seize our priests and kill them all,
>     Kyrie Eleison.

# VI

## The Feast of the Visitation of Mary

Saints in heaven were honored on earth by feast days. Most saints had a single day, some had two. But the Virgin Mary, as suited her position as the Queen of Heaven, had seven feast days. Throughout the Middle Ages, people celebrated the Virgin's Birth (September 8), Purification (February 2), Annunciation (March 25), and Assumption (August 15): one feast day for each season of the year. During the fifteenth century, to match the great upsurge in Marian sentiment that swept over all Europe, there were added three more feast days: the Engagement of Mary (January 23), the Offering of Mary in the Temple (November 21), and the Visitation of Mary (July 2).

The Visitation refers to a passage in Luke (1:36–45) in which the young, pregnant Mary "visited" Elizabeth, an old, erstwhile barren woman, who now also was miraculously pregnant. In Elizabeth's womb was the future John the Baptist, who leapt for joy in the womb at Mary's greeting to Elizabeth. The fetal John announced Jesus the Messiah through his movement, and "Elizabeth was filled with the Holy Spirit." In the later Middle Ages, the Franciscan friars treated this moment as worthy of a feast day: Mary's visit marked for them a special moment of ecstatic joy that heralded—and heralds—a new messianic age. The old age is over. A new age, one of renewal, hope, and the outpouring of the Holy Spirit, begins.

In 1444, the Council of Basel agreed with the Franciscans and fixed the date of the Feast of the Visitation of Mary on July 2. It was to mark annually a time when the old days of bondage in sin and misery would end and a new age of spiritual liberation would begin. On church walls and canvases throughout Europe, painters made the Visitation one of their most popular themes. July 2 was a special day, a day when Mary might again visit the earth and bring liberation to all poor Christians.

Her spokesman on July 2, 1476, was the Drummer, Hans Behem, whom the Virgin had already visited and instructed to preach liberation.

To his followers, Hans Behem was not the Drummer. He was "the Prophet," "the Holy Youth," "Our Good Tidings of Joy." He was the Chosen Son of Heaven through which the Mother of God spoke to her people. And on the obscure little village of Niklashausen shone a beam of heavenly grace. Those entering the sacred light received divine help for their physical and spiritual miseries. From all over Germany peasants came to Niklashausen to bathe in the healing light of the Virgin and to hear her prophet. In Niklashausen was formed a new "classless community" in sacred space and sacred time.

Hans had been preaching for about two months before he gave his sermon on the Feast of the Visitation of Mary. From the beginning he seems to have had the permission, if not the encouragement, of the local parish priest of Niklashausen. Strangely, we know nothing of this man, not even his name. But he allowed Hans initially to preach in the Frauenkirche in Niklashausen until the church could no longer hold the huge crowds of pilgrims. Hans then moved outside to preach from rooftops and windows.

Hans knew his audience well. He knew their fears, their desperate cravings for certainty, salvation, and an end to misery. Other preachers before him, such as John Capistrano, had preached the glories of poverty. Now a shepherd boy, who was the voice of the Virgin herself, preached the same message—but in the down-home dialect of Franconia. Hans was a prophet of the peasants. When we hear him, we hear the peasants of Germany speak.

On July 2, the Feast of the Visitation of Mary, Hans Behem delivered his sermon to perhaps 10,000 to 30,000 people—according to Chronicle estimates. The crowds were so large that he had to preach from a roof window overlooking the village square. How Hans could be heard by all is an interesting question, but one without an answer.

In the crowd were certain men who made a point to hear Hans. They were the spies sent by the authorities of Würzburg and Mainz to note what the Drummer said, at least those statements that could be used against him.

Hans addressed the crowd below, shouting his sermon slowly to be understood, and perhaps addressing the peasant-pilgrims as brother and sister:

> Today, brothers and sisters, is the Feast of the Visitation of Mary. We rejoice today in a new beginning to our lives just as the Blessed John the Baptist rejoiced in his Savior. . . . As you have come to Our Lady here in Niklashausen, so shall you find a new beginning. As you rejoice in me today, so does the Mother of God rejoice in you. For on this holy day, the Mother of God visits you and speaks to you. I am only her humble servant. I speak only as she commands.
>
> You have heard—have you not?—that the Mother of God talks to me. It is strange, some say, that she should talk to a fool who banged a drum and sang foolish songs for all to laugh at.

Yes, yes. I did play, I danced, I sang silly songs. Some of you saw me then. You laughed with me. I *was* a fool: a real fool in life as well as a play fool at the festival plays. I wore bells and the ears of an ass—but I wore them year-round. Why? Because I had danced to the tune of the Evil One. He even came to my lonely pastures to tempt me. But, brothers and sisters, the Evil One is in your villages and towns as well. Did you not laugh with me? Did you not dance and sing and guzzle wine and decorate your bodies as I did? Were you not like the Jews who danced and sang and worshipped the golden calf while Moses went up the mountain to receive the laws of God? They too were filled with the devil. Moses and the true God, however, were filled with anger. You have heard that the she-devil Salome danced before King Herod, and she asked for the head of John the Baptist, the same Blessed John who announced our Savior Jesus Christ at the Visitation. So our prophets have spoken: "Wherever people dance and leap about, there is the devil." God did not give us feet to dance with the devil.

Who among you are followers of the Evil One? For the devil has a flail in his hand which he swings wildly about, and we must dance. But this is our test, don't you see? For as the flail separates the grain from the chaff, so are the saved souls separated from those who are lost to everlasting damnation and fire. The Blessed Virgin says that the Father in Heaven is angry, and he will burn you, and you, and, yes, even you, in fires that never die—unless you cast off your arrogance and your selfishness.

Yes, God is filled with terrible anger. And the gentle Mother of God, who loves us so, pleads with us and warns us, that we must turn aside God's wrath. For today, a day in which the Mother of God should rejoice at the new beginning, today the Mother of God weeps. On the day that we celebrate her joy, she weeps. She weeps for you. She weeps for the world.

We have had our warning from God. Do you remember, my brothers and sisters, last winter the great snows and fierce cold sent by God to punish mankind? The snow was so deep that you

thought that you would not get into the fields to plow, and that
the vines would not produce fruit. You feared that you would
have no fodder for your beasts, and that they—and you—would
face hunger. Do you remember how the wrath of God was going
to bring us to our knees with starvation? We all know that there
was still snow in the fields as late as Cross day [May 3, the Feast
of the Finding of the Cross; since 1960 no longer celebrated].
But I, I with my prayers to the gentle Virgin, turned away the
anger of God. He then gave us warmth. But for how long, my
brothers and sisters? How long can we stay the anger of God?
How long?

We want the mercy of God. But where can we find it? Here,
only here in the Tauber Valley can we find complete mercy
[*volkommen gnade in Tauberthall*]. You need not go to Rome for a
Jubilee indulgence. God's grace is here in the Tauber Valley,
more so than in Rome or any other place. I tell you—no, the
Mother of God tells you—that whosoever sets foot in this blessed
valley will attain complete forgiveness and mercy. Not forty days,
as the priests say if you give them money. But complete forgiveness, as the Holy Virgin says.

Fear not, my poor friends, that you cannot fit into the small
Frauenkirche here in Niklashausen to visit the shrine of Our
Lady. The shrine, like her chapel, is small, but the spirit of Our
Lady is here today—right here in Niklashausen—and engulfs us
all. Can you feel her presence? Yes, yes, you can feel her gentle
warmth. She is here today, and she says that you all will find
grace, forgiveness, and mercy in Niklashausen, beyond the mere
walls of the parish church.

You fear for your own salvation. Of course. Who does not?
But you also fear for your loved ones who might burn in hell. Not
purgatory, mind you, which the priests invented to get your
money for indulgences, but hell. You grieve for the souls in hell.
Grieve not. For I tell you—no, the Mother of God tells you—
that I will lead those poor souls from hell with my own hand, this
hand, just as the Blessed Virgin's Son broke down the walls of

hell to save the souls of the damned from the grip of Satan. With my own hand I will do it.

Trust in the Virgin, honor the Virgin, on this her day of rejoicing.

Let me tell you a story that I heard from a barefooted preacher [an Observant Franciscan]: There once was a poor, little woman who deeply loved the Virgin Mary—not unlike many of you here today. On her table she had a picture of the Virgin and adorned it piously with roses and lilies and other sweet flowers. It happened, however, that her only son had been captured by a powerful lord—yes, you know what I'm talking about: the man had been hunting in the forests of his lord—and was sentenced to be hanged. The woman approached the portrait of the Blessed Virgin with a grieving heart and begged the Virgin to restore her son to her. And because she wanted to regain her son as soon as possible, she pleaded with the Virgin, "Do you not help those who serve you when they are in need? I need you now dear Mother of God." So great was her desperation and grief that she acted as if she were insane: "If you do not restore my son to me," she cried, "I will take your son away from you." She violently seized the portrait—like this, with both hands—and was about to fling it away, when, behold, her son was standing next to her. He grabbed her shoulder and said, "What are you doing, mother? Have you lost your senses? Look. The Mother of God has restored me to you." And so, the poor mother gave praise to the Virgin—as we all do today—that she regained her son.

Whatever powerful lords do to us, whatever they inflict for punishment, work, taxes, or tolls, their authority does not come from God. No. No. The Virgin says to trust in her, not in rapacious lords. Honor her on this day. She hears our pleas against those who oppress us.

Who, indeed, is the earthly power that claims to speak for God and to have dominion over our bodies and our souls? The emperor? No. No. No. The emperor is an evil man [*der keyser eyn bößwicht sy*] and is useful only to the pope. He cares not for you, not for those who toil just to survive. Alas, you poor devils [*Ach we, ir armen tübel*]. The emperor should be our protector, he should obey God's command, but he gives to the electors, to the landgraves, to the knights and their servants, to the spiritual and temporal lords, he gives them power over the common folk [*uber das gemeyn volck*] with their tolls, taxes, duties, labor services and other afflictions that oppress us all. *Ach we, ir armen tübel.*

And what do our pastors do . . . but devour their sheep? Haven't the priests enough already, that they must grasp for more, and more, and more? Do they pay their taxes? No, but you do. Do they pay tithes? Of course not. But you do. You toil in the fields as Adam, our first father, was commanded by God. Do priests? No. No. No. The clergy have many benefices to sustain them and nourish them. They *live* by your labor. You have seen them. Or have you? How often does a priest come to your parish church? Maybe once a month, because they are busy collecting tithes and oblations from their other churches—and serving none of them well. Yes, you have seen them . . . but rarely. Only when they have their hands out to collect money from the poor. They do not speak for God, I tell you—no, the Mother of God tells you—they do *not* speak for God. Each priest, if he is to do his job as God ordained, must have no more than one cure of souls, one living, one benefice to care for.

Don't the priests behave like wolves who raid the sheepfold to devour the sheep, rather than like pastors who protect their flocks? What do you do with ravenous wolves? Of course you know. You kill them.

Yes, that's right. And so should we kill the ravenous priests. Kill them all. They know they are in danger. They fear you. Have you seen the terror in the eyes of the priests here in the Tauber Valley recently? I tell you that the time will soon come when they will slink around like this, with a hand on top of their head to cover their tonsure. They will hope that the common people will not recognize them as priests. But we all know who these wolves are. They should tremble with fear today. They should be struck dumb with fear, for they have not cared for their flocks. They have devoured their sheep and have not taken them to pasture. A lamb that is well fed and cared for will gladly give up his wool for his pastor. But a starving sheep can give nothing—and should give nothing.

They complain—the bishop and his officers—that this is a topsy-turvy world when the feet—you who toil—command the head. Well, I say that time now has been set right, as when Adam and his kinfolk all worked in the fields. We are *all* the body: the feet as well as the hands and head and heart. The time is near when those who hunger and thirst—you, you, and you also—will be satisfied. The time is near when those who are weak—you, you, and you also—will receive the earth for your use. *Ach we, ir armen tübel.*

The Blessed Mother of God speaks to you through me. I am her servant. She knows what God wants, she knows God's great anger at the world, she knows His wrath at the insatiable greed of the mighty who have stolen His creation and made it their own possession. Who owns the fish in the water and the beasts in the field that God created for all of us? They belong to everybody. They belong to us all and should be held in common for the use of all. They are not for the exclusive use of the rich and the mighty who fish and hunt at will and take food from your mouths. The woods are not a sanctuary for the wild animals of the lords, animals that wander the land at will to trample your fields and eat your crops. Can you protect your fields? No. Only the lords, with their contemptible privileges can hunt the wild beasts. If you protect your fields from beasts you will be hanged. *Ach we, ir armen tübel.*

Yes, the great temporal and spiritual lords, and the counts and the knights, have so much wealth and food and wine, that the common folk suffer. Think of it. If they, the small number of rich and their servants, did not hoard all the wealth, there would be enough for all the common folk. We need not go hungry. We need not thirst. God has provided fish and beasts and wine and grain for us all. The Mother of God has told me on this her Visitation Day, a day that will bring us to a new age, that God will no longer allow the rich to take food from the mouths of the poor and hungry.

Do not be in awe of princes and bishops for their fancy clothes. Rather you should praise the poor workers who made those clothes. The old prophet himself tells us that the banquets of the rich are cooked in the sweat of the poor.

How then should the temporal and spiritual princes live? Why . . . like the rest of us, of course. There will come a day, my brothers and sisters, when the princes and lords will work for daily wages. Yes. Then we will see what they are worth. Who would hire them to plow, or to spin, or to card? Can you picture a knight stomping grapes for wine, or carrying dung to his fields? Or a bishop shaping the stones to build his palace? They will work for wages like the rest of us.

*Ach we, ir armen tübel.*

So. We have a pope in Rome and an emperor here among the German people. I tell you, my friends, I do not believe in the powers of the pope or of the emperor. My powers come from God, through His Blessed Mother. You have seen my powers at work, you have seen the miracles, the blind who see, the dumb who speak, the dead who live again and who walk among you. You have witnessed these miracles here in Niklashausen. Have you seen the same powers from the pope? From the emperor? No. No. They can do no such thing. And they will not be with you in heaven. Both of them, the pope and the emperor, will burn in the middle of hell. They will burn forever, as they deserve.

But you, my brothers and sisters, can be saved today by the Mother of God herself, the Blessed Virgin. Give yourself to God. You will be saved today. You will not get another chance in purgatory. You cannot lose your sins in purgatory and then enter heaven. There is no purgatory. It a lie told by the pope and the clergy. Why would they invent such a thing, you ask? Why else, but to allow the mighty to live in luxury and sin in this world. They think that they can still be saved after purgatory. No, I do not believe in purgatory. It is a fanciful tale that will bring your souls to the everlasting fires of hell. You must be shorn of your sins, now, your lustful thoughts, now, your puffy sleeves and pointed shoes, now. Now, I say, before it is too late. Purgatory cannot save you. There is only heaven and hell. In hell you may join the pope and emperor. But believers here in Niklashausen will go directly to heaven and your cares and your pains will be washed away forever by the tears of the Virgin. The Mother of God tells you this.

Priests and the so-called learned theologians babble to each other but they know nothing. Don't believe them. They don't speak for God. Just listen to them—if you can stand it. A priest goes out and gives a sermon about his beliefs; then he returns home and sits around with two or three of his colleagues and they fill each other's ears with babble and chatter. And while they chatter on, they assume that things are better than before, just because a priest gave a sermon. It's as if their chirping bird noises—what they call sermons—will make the world better. I would sooner reform the Jews than the clergy or those so-called authorities of the Scriptures. That is how hopeless these babblers are.

The Holy Book, for example, tells us that there can be no divorce of marriage. Yet priests grant divorces all the time through a babble of legal words. No one, I say, can grant a divorce except God.

And what do the clergy do to those who disagree with their chatter? They issue an order of excommunication. *Ach we.* The bishop's excommunication isn't worth a straw. And neither is his absolution. I would rather have a pot of piss poured over my head than have the hand of the bishop laid there for absolution.

But the priests say that I am a heretic. You have heard them. They say that I am a heretic and that they will burn me at the stake. If they knew what a heretic was, then they would know that they themselves are the heretics, and that I am no heretic. They want to burn me—and they will want to burn you. And they will be happy with what they have done—but then they will finish off with you. Fear not. Through me you will be saved.

Through me, which is to say, through the Blessed Virgin, your sins will be absolved. Some of you were with me in the little chapel just outside my village of Helmstadt. Holtzkirchen it's called, that's right. And you saw me grant absolution to one of the pilgrims who knelt before me there. Yes, and then I sent him to your good pastor here at Niklashausen for consent for the man's penance.

My brothers and sisters, you may be saved here in Niklashausen. For the Mother of God will grant more favors here, in this holy spot, in this blessed valley, than anywhere else in the whole world. . . .

Hans Behem didn't preach that sermon. It exists only in my imagination, reconstructed from the sparse notes that the spies of the authorities compiled and notarized after the sermon. I have tried to recapture the tone and the rhythm from other medieval sermons, but have not used the normal scholastic structure recommended to preachers (that is, announce a passage from the Bible, ask three questions concerning its implications, and then answer each question with a series of reasoned arguments supported by references to authorities). The Drummer, or perhaps any lay preacher, would not have been familiar with the scholastic technique. He would have spoken directly to the emotions and desires of his audience, much as the mendicant friars.

The actual report of the spies is simply a list of heretical or treasonous statements that the Drummer made in his sermon. Each statement consists of a single sentence, designed to be used as evidence in court against Hans. The report begins with the assertion that Hans preached continuously before the people [er sich one unterlaß vor dem folck zu predigen], and then follows with nineteen separate allegations. The document ends with an official verification that these

statements and many more [*und noch vil meher*] were spoken publicly
and were heard and recorded by the writer of the document and the
witnesses (who are unnamed).

The statements are almost all written in the third person, in the
words of the spies. Only rarely do we catch a few actual words of Hans
Behem—perhaps the only words of his that we have in this whole
affair. "*Ach we, ir armen tübel*" appears once at the end of the charge
that the emperor gave his authority to lesser lords to tax and oppress
the poor. It seems to have been used as a refrain by the Drummer to
whip up the crowd and drive home with a heavy cadence their misery
at the hands of the powerful. I have used it as a refrain.

Only one other time do we hear the Drummer's voice. Near the
end of the sermon, he tells the crowd what they already know: that the
priests consider him a heretic and wish to burn him. But he tells the
pilgrims that they, too, will become victims of the priests: "The priests
say that I am a heretic and they will burn me. If they knew what a
heretic was then they would know that they are heretics and I am not.
As they burn me, so they burn you. They know very well what they
have done [when they have burned me], and then they will finish off
with you [or an alternate reading: 'and that will turn against them']":
*Item, die priester sagen, Ich sy eyn ketzer und wollen mich verbrennen.
Wusten sy waβ eyn ketzer were, sie erkentten, daβ sie ketzer weren und
ich keyner. Verbrennen sy mich aber, wee inen; sy werden wol innen, waβ
sie gethon haben, und daβ wurt an inen uβ geen.* In this statement Hans
cleverly became one with his pilgrims against the priests by joining
their fate to his.

When the spies heard the sermon, they probably did not take
notes. That would have been too dangerous. They perhaps went to a
safe place and jotted down what they could remember; they had only
to recall offensive statements. At first glance, the list of statements
seems arbitrary, as if anything offensive was recorded as it was remembered.

But as I imagined the sermon and invented a paragraph to enclose
each statement, I detected a certain logic to the list. The Drummer

first claimed his own authority through the Virgin; he then argued against the temporal authority of the emperor and the spiritual authority of the clergy; he next presented his social message of the commonality of waterways and woods; and he concluded by arguing that the pope and emperor would go to hell, but that the pilgrims who followed the Drummer would be saved by authority of the Virgin, and that there was no purgatory. This argument was contained in the first fifteen statements.

The final four statements do not fit easily into the logic of the sermon: Hans' statement that the priests wanted to burn him; his admission that he absolved a man at Holtzkirchen; his claim that the Mother of God favored Niklashausen over anywhere else; and his assertion that excommunication meant nothing (which was joined to his complaint that the priests gave divorces, whereas only God had that power).

I began the sermon with references to dance and Carnival. This was my own invention and not on the list, and recalls Hans' burning of his drum and his call for the bonfire of the vanities. My allusions to dance as the way of the devil came from a fifteenth-century German sermon against dancing.

The early part of the sermon, where Hans establishes his authority through the Virgin, is especially interesting because he sets himself up as the way to salvation. The spies remembered his saying that he could lead a soul from hell with his own hand: . . . *und were eyn sele in der heln, so wolt er sy mit der hant heruβ furen.* This is an allusion to Christ's harrowing of hell and signals to us that "the holy youth," "the prophet," was evolving into a Christ figure with the powers of Christ. Thus he controlled the fate of souls, as well as the weather and the future. He had become divine.

As a divine figure on earth, Hans had to speak against other authorities, such as the emperor and the pope, who also claimed power from heaven as their mandate to rule. I introduced this section with an *exemplum,* or illustrative story, as Franciscan preachers would have done. Neither the story of the woman whose devotion to the Virgin

103

saved her son from execution, nor the barefooted friar appeared on the spies' list; the story comes from a common book of *exempla* used by Franciscans for their sermons.

Hans had to denounce the emperor, who during the fifteenth century was often looked to by common Germans as well as by serious academic writers to bring about the complete reformation of German society, temporal and spiritual. Ever since the Emperor Sigismund led the reforming Council of Constance in the early fifteenth century, many writers saw the emperor as the divine agent to cure all social ills. Indeed, in 1439, an anonymous writer attending the Council of Basel wrote a powerful and long-remembered tract called the "Reformation of Sigismund" *(Reformatio Sigismundi)*, which called on the emperor to bring peace, order, and justice to the empire. The hope for a general reformation of German society as suggested in the *Reformatio* was repeated by many German writers through the early sixteenth century. When we hear Hans call the emperor an evil man *(der keyser eyn böβswicht sy)* and complain that he does not protect common people but allows lesser lords to oppress them with taxes and tolls, we hear a peasant answer to the *Reformatio*.

Hans' argument against the clergy—that they accumulate many benefices and serve none of them well—is interesting because it often was at the heart of the reform movement of the fifteenth-century church. Bishops such as Rudolph of Würzburg made their reputations as reformers by trying to curb such "pluralism" and by trying to stop the unlawful exchange of benefices on a black market among priests. This was a common problem throughout Europe. Coming from the mouth of the Drummer, the complaint shows popular concern as well.

The spies remembered the Drummer preaching that the priests should be killed. How could they not remember it? This is what they had expected to hear. But they added a colorful statement from the sermon that the day would come when priests would cover their tonsures with their hands to avoid being recognized as priests. This same allusion appears earlier in the prophecies of "John of Parma"— an Italian, c. 1300—who also predicted that the coming persecutions of the priests would compel them to hide their tonsures with their hands. Robert Lerner, in an article on medieval prophecy, writes: "This last image [of hiding the tonsure] was so vivid that it recurred in numerous other late medieval prophetic texts." Hans' use of this imagery tantalizingly suggests the influence of the mysterious Beghard, who may have been familiar with mystic, prophetic literature.

Hans, I think, spoke to peasant fantasies when he preached his social gospel that the waters and woods belonged to everybody; and that the rich should be stripped of their wealth "so that we all have enough" *(so hetten wir glich all genugk)*; and that "the time will come when princes and lords must work for a daily wage" *(eβ kompt dar zu, daβ die fursten und hern noch umb eynen taglone mussen arbeitten)*. Historians usually have interpreted this as a millenarian proclamation, but nothing in any of the documents points to Norman Cohn's conclusion that the pilgrimage to Niklashausen was "the pursuit of the millennium." Only if we define millenarianism broadly to mean "a perfect age or a perfect land" that is "imminent" (so writes Sylvia Thrupp) can we see the Drummer's message as millenarian. But then the very breadth of the definition strips it of much meaning. Rather, I think that the Drummer's social message is a peasant fantasy of egalitarianism—of the village, of the culture of poverty—that he and the pilgrims projected onto the larger world. The world writ large for them was a German village.

My imagery of praising those who make fancy clothes, not those who wear them, and of the banquets of the rich being cooked in the sweat of the poor, came from a tenth-century work by Abbot Odo of Cluny (now a saint). It was irresistible, and it captures the tone of moral outrage of another manic shepherd-preacher, the prophet Amos.

Thus Hans as a budding Messiah held in his hands the material and spiritual salvation of his people. As he could free people from damnation, so could he consign the emperor and the pope to hell.

In his most overtly heretical statement, Hans denied the doctrine of purgatory *( . . . er nichts vom fegefuer helt)*. Although purgatory had become dogma at the Council of Lyons in 1274, it took a long time to penetrate to popular sensibilities. Only during the fifteenth century, for example, did the doctrine of purgatory take hold in parts of France. We should not be surprised if it were still a novelty in fifteenth-century rural Germany. In any case, purgatory was perhaps a lively issue in Franconia, because of the many refugees and preachers who fled Bohemia from the Hussite wars and who carried into central Germany their Hussite denial of purgatory.

Hans, therefore, established his own authority and attacked that of the pope and emperor. He alone must be heard, he seemed to be crying out. Not the priests. It was in this context that Hans made his only reference to Jews: that he would sooner reform the Jews than the clergy and scriptural authorities *(er will die juden ee besseren dan geistlichen und schriftrichen)*. This was coupled with a sentence about a priest giving a sermon and then returning to fill the ears of his colleagues with babble that everything is now better. Jews, in fact, were irrelevant to Hans' complaint against priests except to act as an unregenerate foil to an even more unregenerate clergy. The point seems to be that priests falsely assume that their words have im-mediate efficacy—as if real life were like the sacrament of the Eu-charist: a few words and *voilà*, everything has changed. Hans seemed to imply that priests offer mere words, babble and chatter, not action. I think that Hans revealed to us his deep peasant suspicion of the words and language of the powerful—who, in fact, really did control people's lives through words in their law courts, in their written proclamations that were inaccessible to the illiterate, and in their unintelligible Latin religious formulae. For Hans, in his peasant fantasy, a just world is the world turned upside down, where a person cannot be bound to pay taxes, tolls, and duties when a lord merely points to a document and babbles in legalese.

The spies concluded their document with an odd double state-ment: that Hans claimed that he did not believe in excommunication, and that priests severed (or divorced) marriages when only God may break a marriage *(er sagt, der bane sy nichts; und die priester scheiden die ee, dass nymans gethon mag dan gott)*. Why and how did Hans place this in his sermon? I don't know. So I made it part of the sermon on the efficacy of words: priests dissolve marriages by their words when only God can break those bonds. I believe that Hans saw the real damage that words—whether of divorce or of excommunication—can do to the social fabric. They dissolve family bonds, they break up friendships. This, I think, fits with a strong peasant sense of community: a just world is a direct reflection of peasant justice of the village.

Soon after the Drummer's sermon on July 2, troops of pilgrims, driven by the religious fervor of Niklashausen, caused disturbances throughout southern Germany. We have one eyewitness who in a personal letter allows us to glimpse what happened when pilgrims entered his town of Eichstätt, the seat of a prince-bishop to the south of Niklashausen. Our witness is an anonymous clergyman, probably a canon and official in the cathedral of Eichstätt. For him, the pilgrimage amounted to the rowdiness of bands of disrespectful young people (probably teenage boys) and the stupid credulity of the masses.

His account appears in a long Latin letter to an unknown recipient, dated July 21, 1476. He seems to be writing to his superior outside Eichstätt, perhaps far away, because he feels compelled to explain where exactly Niklashausen is located. And he thinks it necessary to repeat what surely must have been common knowledge for miles around: the story and fate of Hans Behem—although the writer never refers to him by name, only as "a peasant youth, an unlettered, common adolescent."

There were rumors, says our witness, that in the church of Niklashausen the dead would rise and many miracles would happen. So thousands of people went to Niklashausen. Our witness says that this affair was so extraordinary that he himself diligently investigated it. This is his story:

> Two Dominican friars came here and declared the aforementioned miracles to be false. These men had hastened to visit Niklashausen, but they saw people rushing there, not as if they were on a pilgrimage, but as . . . what? A common mob on a

journey, perhaps. I tell you the truth that people were hurrying to Niklashausen as if they were frantic and fleeing from an attacking enemy during a war. They said simply that no one could stop them, and that they were compelled to hurry along. Wives left their husbands, children quit their homes, and farmers abandoned their fields. Frequently as many as eight thousand people came to Niklashausen during one day, sometimes ten or fifteen or even sixteen thousand. Among the great multitudes, one could find always ten boys for every adult male.

Thus, the Youth, that is, the aforesaid peasant [*rusticus*] began to preach, asserting that his authority was from God, and that he was able to lead souls from hell. He spoke openly against the pope and the authority of the church, not fearing excommunication, and he even said with impunity that the priests ought to be killed. The hearts of the laity rejoiced at such words, and they even joked about it.

I can describe to you the articles that were prepared by certain notaries public [the document prepared by the spies], but all tend toward the same thing: that all the goods of the entire world ought to be held in common and divided equally among all, and that all authority of superiors is worthless. From these ideas the pilgrims composed a song which they sang when returning to their homes carrying their banners before them:

> O God in Heaven, on you we call
> Help us seize our priests and kill them all.

And so forth.

Thus, they entered Eichstätt, marching through the middle of the streets in troops; then entering the church, they sang their pernicious song in loud voices. This all began so suddenly, and the lord bishop [of Eichstätt] was not here, but in the town of Herriden [by Ansbach]. I had encouraged the vicar and the preacher of the cathedral to resist and oppose such evil behavior—one of whom answered in an impious manner that he would do nothing, so ignorant were they of the justice of God. At these words, of course, I was aggravated, but remained silent, and only with difficulty stopped myself from reproaching them.

One day, however, about a hundred or more pilgrims entered the cathedral singing their hateful song. They even circled the high altar while singing and calling upon God to help them kill all priests. I then entered the church, snatched up a staff, and drove them all from the church. They all fled, with the exception of one of them, who was stretched out on the ground near the church door. No one resisted me except a cook from this city of Eichstätt, who had joined them and invited them to eat at his place. He made an effort to incite them to defend themselves against me, but he could not persuade anybody, and he himself was driven from the church. Needless to say, a report of what took place immediately circulated, not only throughout the city, but also throughout the entire diocese, that I was in such a rage—as if possessed by a demon—that I was able only to be restrained with fetters, and then only with great difficulty by fourteen men. Such a report was carried even to the remotest parts so that even today it is accepted as truth in Eichstätt.

After this happened, our lord bishop returned because a judicial court was to be held [about the disturbance]. In the presence of the council and other officials of the bishop, I said that I was guilty, because the wolf was not even disguised when it had entered into the sheepfold of Christ God; and that no one cried out, but everybody slept, to the great ruin of simple men. His officials were disturbed by these words and the bishop ordered me to be silent. This took place on the Friday [July 5] before the feast of our patron Willibald, whose feast this year is the fourth Sunday after the octaves of Pentecost [July 7].

The next day, namely, Saturday [July 6], the lord bishop, having convened his cathedral chapter, ordered that a sermon concerning what had taken place be delivered to the people on the feast of St. Willibald. And because the preacher of the church was not adequate to do this, I was to preach the sermon in his place. Having been called to be ready, the burden was placed on me. I declined because of the little time to prepare, and for other reasons. But they refused to accept my excuses. Departing the council chambers, they ordered the meeting adjourned. They also ordered that a town crier loudly proclaim that tomorrow, Sunday, no labor was to be done until the divine service of the mass and the sermon were completed. Likewise it was decreed that this order be promulgated in all churches during the morning of that Sunday. There was much talk among the people; for the bishop and his officials had ordered no other person to preach but me. And because I had ejected the pilgrims from the church during the past week, people said that if I should attempt to speak out in any way against the pilgrimage, they would obliterate me with rocks and stones. This opinion grew so much in strength that the bishop and his officers were anxious for me. For it was dangerous to preach—but more dangerous to be silent.

The fatal hour arrived. I ascended the pulpit after having been presented by the bishop to the clergy and all the people, natives of the city as well as strangers. The church was packed to the rafters; it was estimated that about four thousand people were there. I began by citing the gospels and the divine laws from the sacred canons, the beliefs of the holy doctors of the church, and even the imperial laws. Then with the greatest courage I expressed disapproval of what had been done by the young people and tried to convince them that they should live in obedience to superiors; here, I referred to the apostles who lived in obedience to Christ. I concluded by saying that they should believe what is written in the Scriptures since Holy Scripture follows good morals, not the other way around, at least originally insofar as there is interpenetration, etc.; and they should learn concerning the world that it is not possible to live mired in sin without rulers, etc. I began without a salutation, and I concluded without a valediction. After I had spoken for more than an hour, I retired from the pulpit. And in the course of my sermon, I spoke with words that were neither sparing nor awkward, and when I finished, my friends rushed to me. For I had been moderate in the sermon, and it was praised by everybody for being unpretentious. And, sinking to their knees, they asserted that they never heard such a sermon before, and that they had earlier felt abandoned as sheep without a shepherd.

This opinion did not last, for on the next day, over one hundred people hastened back to the same place. Therefore, I caused a Restraint to be imposed, by which the lord bishop ordered that people be restrained from leaving their pilgrimage to enter our church. Such an order was made on the second feast day after the feast of Willibald [Monday, July 8]: he ordered that the keepers of the town gates not allow any pilgrims carrying standards or singing the said song to enter the city. Having done this, the lord bishop left to visit his palace.

The overwhelming opinion of townsfolk was that the pilgrims had been unfairly prohibited from entering the city. So, on the next day, that is, the third feast day [Tuesday, July 9], there came a throng of people, perhaps sixty or seventy of them, carrying a standard and singing as they did before. However, when they had entered the church, I asked them to stop singing, and with many pious words I persuaded them. They responded that they wanted to sing. Then, without respect for the bishop or me, they persisted in their ways and asserted that the clergy ought to be killed. I grabbed and held onto one of them who seemed more stubborn than the others—even though I was alone and he had called his companions to help him. Nevertheless, I forcefully dragged him to my room—which is on the side—and although he resisted I threw him to the ground, and beat him with so many blows that only with difficulty was he able to drag himself up. His companions fled, and I closed the doors to the building. And when I tried to place him in the tower, again he resisted. In return I punished him with blows until he cried and begged for forgiveness. . . .

Concerning the miracles that took place in Niklashausen, two examples that expose them to you as frauds should suffice: a peasant from the village of Roth bei Herrieden—who also is a subject of the bishop of Eichstätt—visited Niklashausen with his neighbors, who claimed that he had been born completely mute. He made only an unintelligible noise, as if this were the only word allowed him. . . . . This same man, when ordered by the bishop of Eichstätt to be led to torture [to test the truth of his claim], asked forgiveness of the bishop and confessed that he had invented this fraud to collect alms.

A deaf mute, who serves in the stables of the lord bishop of Eichstätt, also visited Niklashausen and gave up all his clothing there [at the shrine], and, as usual, with great howling he prayed before the altar. [The writer now drops into the present tense, presumably for dramatic effect.] A report soon spreads that he also has been cured. With over two hundred people he is returned here and is led to the church of Eichstätt with great pomp. Surrounding the man, before and behind him, people assert their support of him and give thanks to the mute, and they praise God and His Mother. A great clamor of shouting and crying is made, especially around my room, and an old man claims that he can speak with the deaf man. The bishop trembles and, before everybody, orders the deaf mute to be led to me, and he is brought forth by his companions. Standing before me, he spits on the ground and, contracting his nostrils, with a wrinkled brow, he strikes hard with his hand under his armpit. I ask his companions, who best understand his sign language from practice, what these signs mean. They answer that he signifies old women by the wrinkled brow and he curses them; and he desires that they should wear [something to cover themselves in the area] underneath the armpit and above the bladders, because they persuaded themselves to give up their clothing at the church of Niklashausen; and he is intensely angry with them and so he spits on the ground. Yet although he is mute, as stated before, nevertheless, malicious people still proclaim him to be cured and to hear him speak. Their number is infinite.

This paper is now filled up. You well understand that I am placed in the greatest danger for now, and today they say that I and not the bishop prohibit such things, etc.

Hans' sermon on July 2 was a crucial turning point in his destiny. The spies now had provided the legal basis for Bishop Rudolph to proceed against him. The next step for the bishop was to seal off Niklashausen from pilgrims. Bishop Rudolph sent copies of the list of the Drummer's nineteen heretical or treasonous statements to princes throughout Germany to alert them to the dangerous, perhaps revolutionary, situation in the Tauber Valley.

On July 4, the town council of Nürnberg, the powerful, independent city located to the southeast of Niklashausen, responded by prohibiting its subjects from the pilgrimage. The next day, Friday, July 5, Elector Ludwig of Bavaria issued a form letter to all his officials throughout Bavaria, recounting the recent events in Niklashausen and forbidding any of his subjects from going there. It was no doubt prepared by the Elector's spiritual advisors. The document noted that the Drummer (Hans is not referred to by name) preached doctrines repugnant to the Holy Church, to Holy Scripture, and to canon law: he taught that the authorities of the church should have no power. Many people, said the letter, had claimed to have witnessed miraculous signs—which were manifestly untrue. The writers of the document assured lesser Bavarian officials, who were to enforce the prohibition, that the signs *really* were not true, a conclusion they supported by reference to "a report by a trustworthy person" (unnamed) who proclaimed the miracles false.

Also some excellent doctors of the Holy Scripture and of canon and civil law from our university in Ingolstadt have given their assessment, which is that the pilgrimage is the work of some simpleminded people who have no power or authority to teach or to preach and who have neither the consent nor the permission of authorities to do the same. The signs are false and unless we forbid people from going on a pilgrimage to Niklashausen, evil and unrest will sweep over the land.

All the Elector's officials were ordered to announce in their respective jurisdictions that no one, whether young or old, male or female, was to go on a pilgrimage to Niklashausen, under threat of imprisonment and possible loss of life and goods.

Further prohibitions over the next several weeks were issued from cities and principalities throughout Germany. Niklashausen, authorities hoped, would be sealed off.

During the tense days after July 2, Hans continued to preach and pilgrims continued to come to Niklashausen. The Drummer knew that the authorities were closing in on him. In a sermon on Sunday, July 7, he said that the Virgin Mary told him that the pilgrims were to return to Niklashausen on the following Saturday, on the Feast of St. Margaret (July 13). They were to leave their women and children at home, and the men were to come armed with weapons. This was a call to arms. The Drummer—no, the Blessed Virgin—cried out for revolution on the Feast of St. Margaret.

# VII
## The Feast of
## St. Margaret

Margaret who?

That's a good question. St. Margaret is a very confusing saint, or better, collage of saints. Her name usually refers to Margaret of Antioch, who reputedly had been martyred during Diocletian's persecutions in the early fourth century. We know that she was honored in the Eastern Church from an early date, and in the Western Church from about the ninth century, when she appears in the martyrology of Rhabanus Maurus. From the twelfth century, St. Margaret's popularity in the West grew enormously. She was especially favored by pregnant women, who invoked her protection at childbirth, and by crusaders. She reached the height of her pop-

115

ularity during the late Middle Ages when she was accepted as one of the Fourteen Holy Helpers—a group of saints, all martyrs, popular in Germany but few other places, who usually appeared together to protect against disease and death.

But who was she? She may have been the Margaret that St. Ambrose wrote about: a fifteen-year-old virgin who preserved her chastity by jumping off a building. Or she may have been the Margaret (or was it Pelagia?), an actress, who had lived a debauched life only to see the light and become a Christian penitent.

The most common legend about Margaret is that she was the daughter of a pagan priest. She became a Christian, was expelled from her home, lived as a shepherdess-preacher, and converted an immense number of pagans to Christianity. One day the pagan governor of Antioch, Olybrius, took her by force to his palace, and tried to rob her of her virginity. She refused his advances and announced to him that she was a Christian. The governor tortured her, but to no avail. She was even swallowed by a dragon—a symbol of the devil—which subsequently burst open to set her free. (In art she is usually pictured killing a dragon with a spear, or emerging from its belly, as a triumph over the devil.) She and her converts were beheaded in the persecutions of Diocletian.

This is all very confusing. Margaret of Antioch may never have existed except as an accretion of pious stories. However, to somebody like the young peasant visionary and warrior Joan of Arc, in the early fifteenth century, Margaret was corporally real. Joan physically embraced her (along with St. Catherine) and heard her sweet, low voice on many occasions. St. Margaret spoke French. (Joan told the judges at her trial that Margaret did not speak English because she was not on the side of the English.) And St. Margaret convinced Joan to retract her abjuration and accept her execution by fire.

Even St. Margaret's feast day is not clear. Our ecclesiastical calendars tell us that her feast day in the West is July 20, and in the East, July 13. But central Germany strangely followed the Eastern calendar, not the Western, and held her feast day on July 13.

So we are left with a martyred saint, a confused identity, and a confused feast time. We may glean her *persona* from this confusion, that she was a young shepherdess who was swallowed into the evil bowels of the governor/dragon only to triumph over evil by her martyrdom.

In 1969, the cult of St. Margaret was suppressed by the Catholic Church.

The atmosphere in the Tauber Valley was tense in anticipation of the next great gathering of pilgrims on Saturday, July 13, the Feast of St. Margaret. Later chroniclers estimated that about twenty to forty thousand pilgrims were in and around Niklashausen by the end of the week. The crush of people was so oppressive and their desire to touch the "holy youth" so great that Hans and a few of his followers and bodyguards had to stay outside Niklashausen in a farmhouse.

Bishop Rudolph had to act before the Drummer gave his sermon the following day. On Friday night, the eve of the Feast of St. Margaret, thirty-four of the bishop's mounted knights rode to the farmhouse to arrest the Drummer. He no doubt had spies among the pilgrims, because his knights knew exactly where to find Hans. The Drummer and his supporters were caught by complete surprise as the knights burst into his bedchamber to arrest him. They seized him, bundled him on a horse, and took him back to Würzburg with scarcely a scuffle. No one was hurt, not the knights, not the supporters. Only one horse was slightly injured. The midnight raid was a complete success.

Hans Behem, the Holy Youth, the Prophet, the Drummer of Niklashausen, was now in the custody of the bishop of Würzburg to await his fate. He disappeared, vanished, into the prison of the bishop of Würzburg on the Frauenberg, and disappears from all contemporary records.

When Bishop Rudolph's knights broke into the farmhouse to arrest Hans, it was as if the heavenly light that had shone on Niklashausen suddenly went out, leaving those who were encapsulated in its warmth now lost in confusion. Real, normal time of daily power and authority broke into the enchanted time of Hans and his pilgrimage in Niklashausen—and the dreamy illusions of peasant fantasies began to fade and recede into the grey German sky.

Our earliest evidence of the arrest of the Drummer comes from Doctor Kilian von Bibra, a member of Bishop Rudolph's staff in Würzburg. It is a sparse account, written on Saturday, July 13, the day after the Drummer's arrest. Earlier, on July 10, the town council of Nürnberg had written von Bibra asking for information on the gathering at Niklashausen, because they were alarmed by the massive number of people in the Tauber Valley. Von Bibra received their request on July 12 and answered the next day.

Von Bibra reassured the council that prohibitions against the pilgrimage had been announced from pulpits everywhere throughout Würzburg diocese. No person was to be allowed to go through the diocese on this particular pilgrimage, and peasants were forbidden to sing their pilgrimage songs. Nevertheless, he said, great mobs of people came to Niklashausen. Formerly they used to carry only banners, now they were carrying weapons. Presumably he meant their work tools: flails, scythes, hammers, and the like. Von Bibra lamented that no one knew where this would all lead.

Almost in passing he told the Nürnberg council that "the layman" (*der leye*, that is, Hans Behem) had been imprisoned and would receive fair judgment. He noted as well that others from the dioceses of Mainz, Eichstätt, and Würzburg, who had feigned miracles to obtain alms, would be arrested or sent back to their homes. Von Bibra also knew of the arrest of a "hermit" who originally had come from the border of Bohemia and who now lived in a cave in a hill near Niklashausen. The hermit, he said, was popularly held to be a very holy man; he, too, was imprisoned at Aschaffenburg.

Von Bibra finally explained to the Nürnberg town council that the heretical articles (prepared by the spies at Hans' sermon) had now been examined by a professor from Heidelberg. Why? We do not know, but presumably von Bibra had to reassure the authorities in Nürnberg that a sound legal case was being constructed against the Drummer. Beyond this, said von Bibra, he knew nothing.

Everything was still tense and confusing for the authorities.

On Saturday morning, July 13, the Feast of St. Margaret, pilgrims in Niklashausen and the surrounding countryside awoke to discover that their prophet—who was to preach that day and who had told them to come armed to the Feast of St. Margaret—had been captured in the secret of the night. He had been taken from them by the very people whom he had preached against. The pilgrims, of course, were wildly angry and confused about what to do next. Many gave speeches urging one course of action, then another course. Throughout the day there was much milling around, and occasionally a pilgrim delivered a fiery speech.

What to do? Who would lead them now?

Our anonymous writer from Eichstätt tells us that "after the Youth was arrested, another peasant arose, brandishing a sword which he claimed the Mother of God gave him. . . . With this sword, he said, he would kill the bishop and clergy of Würzburg, whom he did not fear."

The authorities' greatest fear was that the arrest of the Drummer might be the spark that would ignite the peasants of Germany to a general conflagration.

By the end of the day, new leaders of the peasants had emerged. Not the sword-wielding peasant mentioned above, but five lesser knights—we assume by their names they were all knights—who for unknown reasons were caught up in the peasant movement: Conrad von Thunfeld, his son Michel von Thunfeld, a man from, or "von," Vestenberg (unnamed), and two men from, or "von," Steten (unnamed). We know only that Conrad von Thunfeld was a local knight from Oberschwarzach (by Schweinfurt) and that he became the captain and spokesman for the people. Without the Drummer, a traditional hierarchy seemingly had formed in Niklashausen in which peasants again were led by knights. The pilgrims were returning to normal time of hierarchy and authority.

During that Saturday night on the Feast of St. Margaret, the pilgrims decided to march to Würzburg to demand the return of their Holy Youth. Led by Conrad von Thunfeld, about ten to twelve thousand pilgrims began their journey to the bishop's castle several hours away. Bishop Rudolph, in a subsequent letter to the Elector of Saxony recounting the affair and urging him to forbid any of his people from approaching Niklashausen, said that thirty to forty thousand people were in Niklashausen that Saturday; sixteen thousand of them marched on Würzburg. The bishop's numbers may have been inflated by fear and to convince the Elector to act immediately. About four hundred pilgrims carried burning, long candles. And they sang their pilgrim songs as they wended their way through the night to Würzburg.

Georg von Geich, a canon of the cathedral of Würzburg, recorded that cathedral officials first received word of the large approaching mob of pilgrims at about two in the morning. Authorities in Würzburg had only a few hours to prepare their defenses, for they had heard that the pilgrims were determined to free the Drummer by force if necessary. Bishop Rudolph and his officers went to his walled castle on the Frauenberg to await the assault.

Early Sunday morning, July 14, the swarm of pilgrims approached the stone bridge that led over the Main River to the Frauenberg. They—or perhaps their captain, Conrad von Thunfeld—were met before the bridge by the bishop's marshal, Jorg von Racken (also called Jorg von Gebsettel in some accounts). He asked them what they intended to do. They said . . . but no, let's allow Johann Trithemius, the old abbot in Würzburg, to tell the story as he reconstructed the affair in 1514:

> Coming before the castle of the bishop, which is called Our Lady's Mount [*Frauenberg*], they called out in a loud voice: "Return the Youth to us, return the holy and innocent man, or else we will destroy the fortress and the city." Marvel at the madness of the people and their foolish confidence!

So much were all these people seized by madness—yea, from the greater of them to the lesser—that they believed without a doubt that the fortress would be destroyed if only they came closer to the walls and merely called out the name of the Youth. Thus, urging each other on with a single-minded purpose, they resolved that they would not depart from the fortress until they had their prophet, or else they would destroy it. They placed all their hope and confidence *not* in arms and the machines of war—of which they had few—but in the merits of holiness of their little Hans. It was not possible, in their estimation, that the most Blessed Mother of God, ever undefiled, the Virgin Mary, Mother of Mercy and Compassion, could forsake the Youth in his captivity (a necessary captivity, I say), to whom she often—so he falsely believed—deemed worthy to show herself so compassionately, nay, I say, intimately.

Those who were in the fortress were astounded to find such a great number of people, and at first not knowing who these people were or where they came from, were astonished more than one can believe. At last, when they understood the reasons for the gathering of pilgrims, they forgot their fears and loaded their cannons to shoot at the mob. But the bishop told them not to shoot. He sent to the people gathered below the walls a certain prudent man, one of his confidential advisors [that is, Jorg von Racken, the marshal], along with a few horsemen, to persuade them to desist in their wicked designs to seize the fortress; and to warn them not to become entangled in such a dangerous undertaking without good cause.

The marshal departed the castle on the hill and approached the mob. He asked them what they wanted, where they came from, and why they came. They answered: "We came from Our Lady, Saint Mary, in Niklashausen, whose servant [that is, the Youth, or so they called the wretch] we want to have. Unless you return him to us, we will not depart from here until we set him free with force and demolish this castle completely." In response, the emissary said, "Good friends, in my judgment you are not only behaving foolishly in this matter, but you also may be assured that you are risking your lives if you attempt to take such a fortified castle by storm, because you have neither cannons nor war machines necessary for such a task."

After hearing many and various speeches for and against what the emissary said, some of the mob were persuaded with little difficulty to depart; for they now knew that the city of Würzburg was armed and that all the cannons in the castle were ready to be used against them.

Fear of the castle guns was not the only reason many of the pilgrims left. Other contemporary writers tell us that Jorg von Racken returned to Bishop Rudolph with the answer of the pilgrims, and that the bishop then sent another emissary to try again to reason with them. These are the bishop's own words:

> I sent Conrad von Hutten, a knight and an excellent man to speak to the people and tell them that all those who have sworn oaths of loyalty to the bishop or the cathedral chapter or their retainers, nobles, knights, and squires, that they should remember their oaths and obligations and surrender now.

About two thousand people, according to the bishop's estimates, surrendered to Conrad von Hutten. They said they wanted to cross the Main River to join their lords and escape the mob, but they did not know where to cross because Conrad would not allow them on the bridge into Würzburg. Conrad told them of a place away from the city where they could ford the river—and again warned them against doing harm to the bishop, chapter, or anybody else.

The remainder of the pilgrims—perhaps ten thousand people, twice the population of Würzburg—stayed obstinately where they were.

When his emissary, Conrad von Hutten, had returned, Bishop Rudolph ordered the castle gunners to fire their cannons—but to aim over the heads of the people. He hoped that the terror of the bombardment would drive off the remaining pilgrims.

The gunners fired their first volley—and the pilgrims witnessed a miracle, O Lord, a glorious miracle. The Mother of God herself had shielded them from cannon fire. And so they surged forward under the canopied protection of the Virgin. Nothing could stop them now.

The castle gunners then lowered their sights and shot directly into the crowd. Several pilgrims were killed and many lay wounded. The crowd was driven by terror and ran from the field. Then out of the castle gates and across the bridge rode a large number of the bishop's armed knights, directly into the panicky confusion of the pilgrims, trampling people and running them through with their lances.

Pilgrims scattered in all directions, chased by knights. One group fled to a churchyard in the village of Waldbüttelbrunn, not far from Würzburg. Here they were trapped by a walled enclosure. They turned on the knights and "threw a great many stones at them" (the bishop's version). But the knights easily overran the churchyard, captured many of the pilgrims, and returned them to Würzburg as prisoners.

The peasant assault on the Frauenberg was over.

What really happened outside the walls of the bishop's castle is difficult to sort out. What I have presented above is the most probable sequence of events, taken from several chronicles and letters. There are differences in detail, but from the confusion of accounts we may discern the main outline: the pilgrims came to the bridge and demanded the release of the Youth; the bishop tried to persuade them to go away; one group belonging to the bishop and other local lords departed; the others refused; they were fired upon by cannons and run down by attacking knights; many fleeing pilgrims were trapped at Waldbüttelbrunn and returned to Würzburg as prisoners.

The anonymous writer from Eichstätt said that more than three hundred people were captured in the cemetery of Waldbüttelbrunn, about seventy of whom escaped on the way back to prison. All were held captive in Würzburg, and the prisons and dungeons overflowed. About forty people had to be held in a churchyard under guard. We do not know the true figures. Georg von Geich, a canon of Würzburg cathedral, noted that about a hundred prisoners were taken to the

Frauenberg for questioning. The only "precise" figures that we have are from Konrad Stolle, a Thuringian chronicler writing about 1500, who is maddeningly uneven in his reliability: sometimes his information is simply wrong, sometimes wonderfully precise. He reported that 38 pilgrims were killed that day, and 127 imprisoned.

We know that the peasant assault on Würzburg was over—but Bishop Rudolph did not. He and his officers fully expected another attack on the town or the castle, and so he immediately sent requests to princes and towns all over Germany to urge prohibitions of people going to Niklashausen, to stop the flow of peasants into the Tauber Valley.

On Wednesday, July 17, Georg von Geich read before the town council of Würzburg a report of the current situation in order to urge them to take all necessary measures to prepare for further attacks. Interestingly, he also explained his fear of unrest among the local population of Würzburg, some of whose sympathies were with the pilgrims. Some people in Würzburg, he said, had spoken openly against the bishop and his chapter, saying that if the pilgrims came again they would fight alongside them. "And some women said: Our Grace and His Grace's clergy are vain, evil men; they imprisoned a pious man, the Youth; and Our Lady has authorized her pilgrimage." Von Geich also spoke for the archbishop of Mainz, who "requests that anybody who wishes to go on a pilgrimage not be allowed, for fear that they would bring about a great insurrection."

Every street and alley in Würzburg must have been buzzing with confusing and fearful rumors. Von Geich reported that "there is talk that the Swiss shall come here, and this is widely believed." The peasant-Swiss were the most feared mercenaries in Europe, and the fear in Würzburg was that they would side with the peasant-pilgrims.

What to do? Von Geich requested that nobody be allowed to enter or to leave Niklashausen. It should be isolated as if under quarantine. Above all, nobody—neither men, women, the elderly, nor children— should be allowed to speak the evil doctrines that originated in the pilgrimage or sing the evil pilgrimage songs. The bishop specifically asked through his spokesman, Georg von Geich, that the council be loyal to him and that they provide a hundred horsemen by Friday (July 19), because the common talk was that the pilgrims would come again "to thin the vineyards."

The town council issued orders to follow all the bishop's requests. Naturally. They belonged to the bishop.

In Eichstätt, our anonymous author (writing on July 21) had heard much talk that the pilgrims might return in force but was disdainful of their ability to mount such an attack:

> This you know, that throughout all of this I remain composed and calm, and I was never at any time very frightened. And although all the blind populace rage, they cannot be roused to action; it is as if they were pressed by a most heavy torpor. But still they proclaim they will return to Niklashausen and that all the clergy ought to be killed before the Feast of St. Michael [September 29]; and they treat all this with happy hearts. I am confident that I can defend myself with words and scourges.
>
> We pray to God that He make everything well and He turn His anger from us, because such a struggle to return to normal cannot happen in such a short time without the special help of God.

"We pray to God that . . . He turn His anger from us." This was the same hope of the Drummer and his pilgrims, and a driving force behind the pilgrimage. Of course. The authorities and the rebel-pilgrims shared the same assumptions about the constant and immediate influence on the earth of God and His saints. They disagreed only on how supernatural beings influence humans: whether through lawful authorities or through chosen laypersons.

This was a touchy point for contemporaries who wrote about the pilgrimage (and who were all on the side of the authorities). They had to explain the miracles in Niklashausen. If the miracles were true, then the Virgin indeed may have called the pilgrimage, and the authorities were acting against God's wishes. Their questions about the veracity of the "miracles" and "signs" at Niklashausen reveal to us a nervous subtexture to the whole affair. For example, when the bishop's marshal, Jorg von Racken, appeared before the Würzburg town council on Wednesday, July 17, he specifically argued that the evil uprising of the peasants had originated in one person only, the Drummer. "This affair did not come from God," he reassured the council, ". . . and if all the miraculous signs took place that people say took place in Niklashausen, then they would amount to more miraculous signs than had ever taken place under our God and all his saints. They were all vain inventions and false roguery." Marshal Jorg then regaled them with a story he had heard from the bishop of Eichstätt of a conspiracy by some men to send one of their number to Niklashausen pretending to be a mute; when he got there he was to speak "miraculously" in order to obtain alms.

Bishop Rudolph, himself, in a letter to the Elector Wilhelm of Saxony, recounted the arrest of the Drummer, and assured the Elector that "no signs took place."

We are observing minds of the elite that were not far removed from those of the pilgrims. The authorities, like the peasants whom they despised for their ignorance and superstition, constantly watched the heavens and the natural world for divine signs, for clues to discern the wishes or the mood of God. Is He happy today? Is He wrathful? (God was generally wrathful, because something was always awry in the world.) The pilgrims saw the signs through their prophet Hans, the Holy Youth, and the signs told them that God was angry with the entire ruling class of Germany. German authorities, therefore, were predisposed to attack the miraculous signs in Niklashausen as false, fraudulent, and feigned.

In account after account, writers dwelt on deceitful cases in which the dumb supposedly spoke, the dead raised, the blind restored sight. They did not doubt that such miracles could take place, only that they had taken place in Niklashausen. They were forced to be skeptical, not of divine signs in general, but of these signs in particular. God had to be on the side of the rulers. The legitimacy of the social, political, religious, and economic structure of Germany rested on the fraudulence of the "miraculous signs." What if . . . just what if the signs and miraculous cures were true? God and His Mother would be calling for a world turned upside down, a Carnival world in earnest. No, the signs had to be false. The advantages of proofs, logic, and publicity in the battle over miracles all lay with the authorities against the pilgrims.

When Bishop Rudolph, his officers, and his knights peered over the walls of the Frauenberg, they saw only *das gemeyn folck:* the common folk, or the mob, or the crowd, or the gathering, or the multitudes. Consequently that is all we are allowed to see of the thousands of people who gathered by the stone bridge that led to the Frauenberg on that Sunday morning in July. We see abstract numbers, twelve or fourteen or sixteen thousand people, and four or five hundred candles. The abstract *gemeyn folck*.

Fortunately, one document, which contains some information about the "confessions" of a select few of the prisoners held in the Frauenberg, has survived and is worth quoting in full. For a fleeting moment a few people come into focus—but only through the eyes and questioning of their enemies in the ecclesiastical establishment. The document was prepared for Archbishop Dieter of Mainz, who presumably conducted the investigation because Niklashausen lay in his diocese. It is unclear to whom he is reporting, if anybody. We may be looking at a synopsis of the investigation for the archbishop's files. It was produced sometime during the week of July 14 to July 18, and focuses on alleged miracles, which seem to have been the primary concern of the investigators.

Item, they said about a child that had drowned, that he was taken to Niklashausen, and was brought back to life again. There was nothing divine about this, but rather the child had fallen into the water and his father quickly came to his help so that he did not die. Therefore, he had not been brought back to life.

Item, they said about a man from Ostheim [Grossostheim bei Aschaffenburg?], that for a long time he had been lame but his legs were made straight [at Niklashausen]. There was also nothing divine about this, because he had moved before in the same way that he still moves.

Item, they said about a child from Krotzenberg [Grosskrotzenburg bei Hanau?], that he had been born blind but now could see. This is also not true [that is, divine], because the child has always had weak eyesight, and has it still.

Item, they also spoke of a man who was born a mute, that he began to speak there [at Niklashausen]. We have this same man in prison now. He has confessed that he received much money for this; and that he and a companion joined together to have people think that he was a mute in order to obtain money. And he went with a number of people along the way on the pilgrimage and said nothing until they came to Niklashausen, where he began to speak. Because of this deception, he obtained some money and the people wept over him as if he had been a mute. Thus, the common folk [*das gemeyn folck*], who had come in good trust and hope to venerate the Virgin Mary, were led astray.

Note that the four examples deal with four different supposed miracles: raising the dead, and healing the lame, the blind, and the mute. These appear to be "types" of fraudulent miracles which were used to disprove all miracles at Niklashausen.

The thrust of the document now shifts to other supposed miraculous happenings:

Item, a Beghard Brother who lived in a mountain also came to that place [Niklashausen]; and we now have him in our custody and prison. [This is the same man who presumably was Hans' teacher and with him in Niklashausen, and the same man whom Kilian von Bibra said had been captured with Hans and taken to Aschaffenburg.] He had lived for a long time in the mountain and now for the first time has come out; just as a spring has its source in a mountain, so is it now the case. [The scribe now seems to paraphrase the enigmatic testimony of the Beghard.] The same Beghard Brother said among other things that the spring flows through the night to feed into a river;

therefore, so should a light be placed before a mountain in the night; and he has lit that light. Thus, everybody [that is, the investigators] stopped to remark, that because of that light, the common folk have all been enticed to travel and to be led astray. And just as the Drummer (so men call the Youth) has been captured, so also the Beghard wants to free him; he has been seized and is now in our hands.

Item, so have we captured and imprisoned the priest [of Niklashausen, unnamed]. He said—indeed, he confessed—that he had preached concerning a great many miraculous signs and miracles as if they had actually happened, when in fact he had no knowledge about them.

Item, a peasant cut off the hair of young maidens. That is forbidden by law and by pain of excommunication, and is permitted only to cloistered maidens in convents. [That is, common maidens were being turned into holy women fraudulently by authority of a common peasant.]

Item, they said concerning three young maidens that they had been drowned, and then come back to life. This is not divine, because they were dead and not brought back to life. They were also buried.

Item, after the peasant, the man they call the Youth [that is, Hans the Drummer], was imprisoned, another peasant arose and said strange and unchristian things, and he also preached. All that he preached was against the order of the Holy Christian Church and against us, as archbishop, in whose diocese Niklashausen lies. [This may be the same peasant whom the anonymous writer of Eichstätt mentioned who brandished a sword and claimed visions of the Virgin.] We cannot tolerate these opinions any longer, but will do what is proper against them; and so that the opinions will not incite an uprising, we intend and resolve to put a stop to this pilgrimage and treat this whole affair with severity.

Who should be treated "with severity"? Who exactly was responsible for the massive pilgrimage and the abortive uprising? This is what the authorities wanted to know now that they had the Drummer and more than a hundred of his followers in custody. For an answer, we must rely on contemporary observers of the affair, the ecclesiastical authorities and the Drummer's enemies. Even they were not sure.

By the time that the authorities met at the end of June to deal with the Drummer, they knew of others who might be helping him. They had heard of a "preacher monk," that is, a Dominican friar, who also was preaching heresy at Niklashausen. The authorities did not know then, nor do we know now, who the Dominican friar was or how prominent a role he actually played. He may have been a renegade friar, attracted by the explosive conditions at Niklashausen. We have no reason to believe that he was Hans' teacher or that he manipulated Hans behind the scenes. We do not even know whether he was really a Dominican.

The man who witnesses thought was a Dominican may have been the mysterious Beghard Brother—dressed similar to a friar—who was with Hans in Niklashausen and who may have been with him from the beginning. He lived in a cave in a hill by Niklashausen and perhaps talked with, and instructed, the young shepherd Hans in the solitude of the shepherd's fields. We have seen that the Beghard Brother confessed in mystical, allegorical language that he was a light in the night, or a stream that flowed during the darkness to feed a great river. He confessed, in other words, that his light would guide those who were lost to the truth, that from his lonely cave would flow inexorably in the night—unseen to authorities—the waters of salvation. The Beghard Brother may have been mistaken for a friar. In any case, he was captured with Hans and was known to authorities as a dangerous threat: investigators implied that he was the cause of the affair, "just as a spring has its source in a mountain, so is it now the case."

What about the parish priest of Niklashausen? Surely he must have had something to do with the whole affair. But we do not hear of him until after Hans' arrest and the pilgrims' march on Würzburg. When he was arrested, he confessed only that he had preached about the many miracles that had occurred in Niklashausen, when, in fact, he had no real knowledge of them. As close as he was to all the events in Niklashausen, the parish priest seems to have been a minor figure. We may imagine that initially he encouraged the visionary shepherd to preach and to call for a pilgrimage to his church, which would enrich him through the pilgrim's offerings, but that he was relegated to a bit part in the drama as the pilgrimage became increasingly radical and out of control.

There were those who led the assault on Würzburg. But even they are shadowy. On July 15, Doctor Kilian von Bibra, in a report to a colleague in Nürnberg about the previous day's pilgrims' march to Würzburg, casually mentioned in a postscript that the "captains" of the people had fled. They were Conrad von Thunfeld, one (man) von Vestenberg and two (men) von Steten *(Contz von Thünfelt, einer von Vestenberg und zwen von Steten; die sein fluchtig worden).*

That we know anything at all about Conrad von Thunfeld is because on October 25, 1476, several months after the assault on Würzburg, Conrad and his son Michael made peace with Bishop Rudolph, as recorded in two documents. The first is an admission by the von Thunfelds, father and son, that they led the common people on their march to Würzburg to free the Drummer, followed by an oath to keep the peace. To ensure their loyalty and peaceful behavior, Bishop Rudolph forced them to sign another document, in which the von Thunfelds turned over to the bishop their hitherto freehold land, only to receive it back as a feudal fief. The price of their dabbling in the popular pilgrimage was expensive. They lost their land and would forever be vassals to the bishops of Würzburg. They had held three houses, two forests, two vineyards, and several bits of property, all near Schweinfurt, and all of which now came under the lordship of the bishop of Würzburg.

Considering that they had led a rebellion, the von Thunfelds got off easy. So did almost everybody else who participated in the assault. After a brief period, Bishop Rudolph emptied his prisons and dungeons of pilgrim-prisoners and sent them home. We do not know when he freed them, but it was probably after the immediate threat of an anticipated second assault on the castle had passed.

Three men were not spared: the Drummer, the Beghard Brother

with a long beard, and the peasant (a miller) who had claimed visions from the Virgin after the Drummer's arrest and who had waved a sword proclaiming death to all priests. For them, the enchanted time was over. Locked away in the Frauenberg, interrogated by earthly powers, they no longer were engulfed in the warm glow of a heavenly beam. Life returned to normal time, a time of authority, power, and social order.

Between Monday and Friday, July 15–19, Hans Behem stood trial for heresy. The Beghard Brother and the peasant-miller perhaps were also tried—but for what? Probably treason. We don't know.

We do not have Hans' trial records, nor do we have a contemporary description of what took place. We know that Bishop Rudolph had collected statements of notarized witnesses and expert judgment from university professors, presumably to be used in court. And all chroniclers tell us that Hans Behem was convicted of heresy by Bishop Rudolph.

The bishop's marshal, Jorg von Racken, apparently attended Hans' interrogation. He reported to the Würzburg town council about July 16 or 17 that "with his words he [the Drummer] set in motion several thousand people, and for fear of his life he laughed at everything. It was not so with the twelve apostles and other holy martyrs: what they said they did not deny and they died for their faith." Jorg seems to have meant that Hans tried to deny what was charged against him at his trial or interrogation and laughed about it as a joke.

We know enough about ecclesiastical courts to reconstruct what probably took place in the bishop's court. Hans' apparent denial was not given in open court, but rather under interrogation, which was a part of the trial procedure. That is, he probably made his denial under torture or the threat of torture.

This requires a brief explanation. The legal procedures used in Hans' heresy trial followed a rigid hierarchy of proofs. In canon law procedures, witnesses were important to prove a crime, but not so important as in, say, English common law procedures. In canon law (as in Roman law) the most important proof was the "spontaneous confession" of the accused. If two sworn and notarized witnesses testified against the accused, then a confession was not necessary. Nevertheless, jurists and canonists had justifiable doubts about the reliability of witnesses and turned to confession as the irrefutable proof of guilt; confession, they said, was the "queen of proofs." The accused must convict himself by his own mouth. Judges alone decided cases (there were no juries in canon law courts), and confession spared judges from making difficult decisions; a "spontaneous confession" greatly eased their consciences.

Since a confession was considered crucial for a guilty verdict, medieval courts that used Romano-canonical procedures (that is, canon law and Roman law procedures) did what was necessary to extract confessions, including torture as a last resort. But torture was used only in cases where the penalty was death or mutilation, and when the truth could not be found by other means. It was a procedure to be used when all else failed.

Jurists realized, of course, that people would confess anything under torture, that a confession under duress was not spontaneous, and, therefore, not legally valid. Thus they said that a defendant who confessed under torture must repeat his confession "freely," after one day's waiting, in open court. This was the "spontaneous confession." It was also a legal fiction: for if the accused retracted his confession in court, he was then sent back to be tortured, and his recantation was now an additional charge against him.

By the fifteenth century, because of widespread heresy in Europe, procedures in heresy trials had come to favor prosecutors with extraordinary measures: the accused was not necessarily informed of the names or the testimony of his accusers; testimony of biased, normally ineligible witnesses was allowed; normal rules of evidence were relaxed to give greater weight to facial mannerisms and the nervousness of the accused which might indicate guilt; and the court was allowed to deceive the accused with false promises of leniency in return for information.

Hans was tortured in the most common way, *per cordam,* "by the rope." This torture was the "queen of torments," which virtually guaranteed confession, the "queen of proofs." Or so said medieval jurists. Hans' hands were tied behind his back with a long rope which was draped over a ceiling beam. He was then raised off the ground, his body weight tearing at his shoulders and back. Hans could have been raised or lowered any number of times until he told his torturers what they wanted.

Abbot Johann Trithemius perhaps had access to the bishop of Würzburg's archives when he wrote his account of the Niklashausen affair and may have seen the trial or torture records:

> Next, the swineherd drummer, the youth, little Hans, the false prophet of the people, the captive deceiver, whose prophecies the common people held to be the truth, was interrogated by the rope [*per cordam*] and he confessed that everything was fictitious, false, and feigned. And with a free voice [*voce libera*], he said that a wandering, cunning mendicant friar had contrived everything. Later when this same friar heard that the little fool had been captured, he saved himself by fleeing as far away as possible.

This is the only evidence that Hans was tortured.

But why torture the Drummer? Bishop Rudolph had notarized witnesses against Hans and had ample proof of his heresy. But he needed irrefutable proof, a confession. That's what he wanted. He wanted to hear from the Drummer's own mouth that he (and a conspirator) made the whole thing up, that the miraculous visions did not really happen. The bishop and his clergy had to soothe their own fears that the heavens might have opened to the shepherd; and they had to publicize the "fraud" to others. They also had to make sense of what had happened at Niklashausen by reconstructing—or constructing—an explanatory narrative that had a ring of truth: simple, illiterate Hans was not smart enough to concoct so great an affair, and had to have had a devious, educated accomplice, a renegade mendicant friar who fled the region and was never caught. Even if Hans *never* had a friar who was the mastermind of the whole conspiracy, he now had one. The authorities made sure of this with the proof of a freely given confession: "And with *voce libera,* he said that a wandering, cunning mendicant friar contrived everything." This was Hans' "spontaneous confession," presumably the day after he was tortured.

Today we are rightly skeptical about information gathered under torture or threat of torture. And we ought not to accept Hans' implication of a renegade friar in the affair. There may indeed have been a Dominican preaching at Niklashausen, just as the authorities thought when they met at Aschaffenburg, but it is equally plausible that he was a figment of their imaginations. We have no other information about the friar. Hans' confession—if, indeed, he made one—perhaps gave rise to all later interpretations of the mysterious friar who whispered in Hans' ear what to preach.

Hans Behem, the Drummer of Niklashausen, was convicted of heresy and sentenced to be burned at the stake. His two companions, the Beghard Brother with the long beard—who, in fact, may have instigated the pilgrimage—and the peasant-miller, were both sentenced to be beheaded. The executions were to take place on Friday, July 19.

There is a story, or *exemplum,* that Franciscan friars commonly repeated in their sermons. It is a strange story that places love of the Virgin Mary and her miraculous powers above man-made law and social values. The moral seems to be that the Mother of God will protect those who are especially devoted to her, even from the judgment of authorities, even from death. Perhaps Hans had such a story in mind as he was led to the stake singing with a loud, high-pitched voice the hymns that he had composed to the Holy Virgin.

There was once a man named Ebbo, who often robbed others of their goods, which he carried away by stealth. And yet he truly venerated the Holy Mother of God with all his heart; and when he was in the act of robbery he was especially devout in his reverence for her. One day, however, when in the act of stealing, he suddenly was apprehended by his foes, the authorities. Because he was unable to purge himself by producing the required number of compurgators, he was judged by the court to be hanged by the neck until dead. And so he was led to the noose without mercy and without delay. He was hanged; his feet were suspended in the air.

But behold! The Holy Virgin Mother came to his aid, and supported Ebbo in the air, protecting him from harm.

Two days went by and those who had hanged Ebbo returned to the place where they had left him hanging. They saw him alive, with a cheerful expression on his face, as if nothing had happened. In their astonishment, they took off the noose that had been tied around his neck, and inspected his windpipe. It had not been cut by the rope! They now understood that they could not harm Ebbo because the Virgin Mary had placed her hands near his windpipe to protect him. Indeed, they realized that the Holy Virgin would protect him from harm, and so they dismissed Ebbo by the love of God and His Mother. Ebbo then became a monk, and afterward for as long as he lived he served God and His Most Holy Mother.

For our fullest account of what happened at the execution of the Drummer and his companions, we again must turn to Abbot Johann Trithemius:

Certainly, there were those who with imprudent faith believed that his whole affair originated in heaven. And in the city of Würzburg there were many such people who were intensely afraid to take part in the execution of the Youth. Moreover, even if the Youth were dragged to the stake, they hoped that God would preserve him from being killed; or if God allowed him to die, then He would take immediate vengeance on the courts that condemned the Youth. Others, who were more sane, among whom were the bishop and his clergy, did not fear the vengeance of God for the death of this wicked man; rather, they earnestly, sensibly, and rationally feared that spiteful, evil spirits—who take delight in possessing superstitious people—would scheme some plot of guile and deceit at the execution. For they judged that little Hans was not a man of God but was possessed by the devil.

At last the judgment of death to little Hans was to be carried out. . . . After he had been led to a level piece of ground, which is behind my monastery near the house of the lepers, he was seated and bound with ropes. Nearly all the citizens of the town stood by armed, waiting for him to be delivered to the fires. In the meantime, two evildoers who were with him received a sentence to have their heads cut off. After they were beheaded, little Hans said to the magistrate: "Are you going to hurt me?" The magistrate replied: "No, but someone has prepared a bath for you"— for the Youth had not yet seen the pile of wood for the fire, or if he had seen it, he perhaps did not know what it was.

When he was tied to the stake for burning, however, he sang certain songs or verses in a high voice about Our Lady, which he had composed in the German language. Among the bystanders were many who believed that the man could not be burned because of the merit of his holiness, by which they thought he would be preserved by the Mother of God. Hence, they were afraid to stand near him. They were terrified that perhaps the fire would be scattered about by divine fury and would consume those observing the execution. Others feared that the Youth could not be burned because of the protection of demons or of some other sorcery. Therefore, the executioner—who also feared this— caused all the Youth's hairs to be shaved, so that no evil spirit or demon would be able to hide in them.

Bound to the post, the Youth shouted his songs. But as soon as the fire was set below him and he felt the flames, he cried out three times with a weeping voice: "Ow, ow, ow." He was then engulfed by the flames. His voice uttered nothing again. Consumed by the voracious fire, he was reduced to ashes. No miracles happened, nothing that demonstrated that Innocence had been consumed by fire. Nevertheless, so that the frivolous devotion and fear of stupid people not fashion him into a martyr, the executioner ordered that all his ashes be thrown into the river. After this was done, the gathering of the people at Niklashausen came to an end.

# VIII

## Historical Time

The pilgrimage to Niklashausen as a mass movement, indeed, had come to an end. But contemporaries did not know that, and for weeks after the Drummer's execution, authorities in Würzburg continued to maintain their defenses against another expected assault by the peasant-pilgrims. Water buckets were ordered to be refilled, not only because the old water was beginning to stink, but also in anticipation of fire from a peasants' war. The assault never came. Massive numbers of peasants who had trooped to Niklashausen now trooped home.

The execution of the Drummer, however, was not the end of the affair. In Würzburg, some secret followers of the Drummer dug up dirt from the spot where he had been burned and preserved it as a sacred relic or as magic powder, perhaps similar to the ashes they collected from the regenerative Easter bonfires. In Niklashausen, pilgrims still came to the church, not in gangs as during the summer, but they came. The spot where the young prophet had preached was for them a blessed site.

Authorities in Würzburg, Nürnberg, and other cities and principalities for the next two months issued and reissued to their subjects prohibitions from visiting Niklashausen. In mid-September, Archbishop Dieter of Mainz wrote to Count Johann of Wertheim urging him to stop pilgrims from going to the place where the Drummer had preached. Bishop Rudolph made the same request to the count on September 20. Count Johann took the moral high ground in his reply to the prelates: he lectured them on the benefits of pilgrimage to the souls of his subjects, and reminded them that Niklashausen, after all, did have a papal letter that confirmed it as a pilgrimage church. He also remarked off-handedly his real concern, that he was reluctant to ban the movement of pilgrims through his lands because of the revenues pilgrims brought in. At least the count held a consistent position: banning tourism is bad business.

Still pilgrims came to Niklashausen. Not in great numbers, but they came.

Archbishop Dieter, on October 10, used his authority against Count Johann; he placed the church of Niklashausen under interdict and repealed its powers to grant indulgences. In his decree he rehearsed the role of the Drummer ("a peasant, ignorant, worthless, untrained in knowledge or morals") and argued that because the common people chose to listen to him, they were to be cut off from the shrine and indulgences of Niklashausen. The archbishop then added an odd statement that has antifeminine overtones: from the very beginning of the affair in Niklashausen, he claimed, the lewd dances and drum playing of the pilgrims incited girlish play and feminine allurements, which are not the distinguishing marks of Christians, but of the devil. For an instant we are allowed to glimpse into the strange fantasies of the archbishop. What did he think took place in Niklashausen?

Yet pilgrims came to Niklashausen. In secret, perhaps at night, but they came.

For Archbishop Dieter, the errors that had been seminated at Niklashausen were "weeds" that had to be eradicated. He knew that the pilgrims still came, and he knew why they came: for the "false rewards" of eternal glory and salvation promised by the Drummer to anybody who made a pilgrimage to the church. They came despite the interdict. There was only one thing to do: destroy the church building itself, raze it to the ground, and obliterate all physical traces—just as the Drummer had been obliterated. By order of Archbishop Dieter, no portion of the church was to be reconstructed after its demolition. The cure of souls attached to the church was transferred to the parish of Gamburg. In the early months of 1477, the church of Niklashausen was eradicated from the earth. There were to be no reminders of the great pilgrimage of the Drummer of Niklashausen in 1476. The peasant fires finally were extinguished.

The authorities had triumphed, and now was the time for them to congratulate each other. Of the many congratulatory letters that crossed southern Germany, those which have survived are in the Nürnberg archives. On February 7, 1478, twenty months after the death of the Drummer, Pope Sixtus IV sent the town council a letter of appreciation for their actions to halt the pilgrimage to Niklashausen. The papacy had been informed of Nürnberg's response to the crisis by Doctor Kilian von Bibra, the provost of Würzburg, and so, on March 26, 1478, the town council of Nürnberg sent a letter of appreciation to von Bibra for informing the pope on their behalf. All the major figures among the authorities had their appropriate letters— nice souvenir letters with fancy signatures and seals—of mutual appreciation for having put an end to the Drummer.

What happened to all the money and goods that pilgrims piously had left in Niklashausen as offerings to the Blessed Virgin? It was divided equally among the bishop of Würzburg, the archbishop of Mainz, and the count of Wertheim. Only by chance do we know what happened to the windfall profits of one of the authorities: Archbishop Dieter of Mainz used his money from the pilgrimage to construct a great wooden arch at his castle. In 1481, his castle burned to the ground, and nervous, popular rumor attributed the fire to God's judgment on the archbishop for his role in burning the Holy Youth.

As the years passed, the whole affair at Niklashausen receded into vague memory, legend, and the mocking scorn of chroniclers and historians. By the turn of the sixteenth century, the Drummer and his extraordinary pilgrimage now existed only as a didactic *exemplum* for preachers, historians, and moralists. Sebastian Brant singled out the Drummer for a special spot on his Ship of Fools: he used the madness and the novelty of the Drummer and his pilgrims at Niklashausen to instruct educated readers—as if they needed instruction—of the fickle stupidity of the masses who would follow an uneducated, illiterate half-wit such as Hans.

By 1518, the memory of the pilgrimage to Niklashausen was no longer a threat to authorities, and on July 26, 1518—forty-two years and one week after Hans' execution—the archbishop of Mainz, Albrecht von Brandenburg, granted permission to rebuild the parish church of Niklashausen. This, of course, was the same Archbishop Albrecht who, in need of money, had pushed hard for the sale of indulgences throughout Germany—indulgences that were to incite young Martin Luther at his university in Wittenberg to challenge scholars to public debate concerning their efficacy. Archbishop Albrecht appealed to all good Christians in his diocese to contribute to the rebuilding of Niklashausen . . . and he granted all contributors an indulgence of 140 days. Thus, in the first days of the Reformation, Niklashausen was restored. It was as if the Drummer had never existed.


Bishop Rudolph, that indefatigable old reformer, continued his reformation of Würzburg—long before the Reformation. The most persistent problem that Bishop Rudolph faced during his long rule was the reform of the convents, which were filled with aristocratic women whose families had used the convents as dumping grounds for superfluous daughters. The women expected to live in their cloisters according to their social rank. They resisted the stringent rules that the bishop tried to impose on them, especially the dress codes and rules to enclose the women from the outside world. Despite prohibitions, the women still wore jewelry; they still made fashionable cuts in their (illegal) puffed sleeves; they still slit open the backs of their habits with chic and sexual provocation; and they still insisted on wearing pointed shoes. Bishop Rudolph never solved the problems in the cloisters although he tried year after year. It was in 1476, the year of Niklashausen, that the bishop issued a new and all-encompassing order for the cloisters—to little avail. The two events are not related, but one suspects that the bishop's problem with the discipline of the cloisters was much more of an annoyance than the problem at Niklashausen. The Niklashausen affair at least had a solution.

How was the reforming bishop to reach the laity, those same folk who had flocked to Niklashausen? From the standpoint of a top administrator, there was little in fact that he could do directly. He could not be everybody's priest. But he could reach people indirectly by ordering his clergy, with their newly printed liturgical books from the Würzburg press, to instruct parishioners on the basic prayers of the church, the *Pater Noster,* the *Ave,* and the *Credo.* Most of the population did not know them, despite their enthusiasm for other aspects of the church.

Teach the people, yet harness their outbursts of enthusiasm for pilgrimages and indulgences—this was Bishop Rudolph's strategy. During the late fifteenth century, huge numbers of people periodically left their fields and workplaces to go to a holy shrine to seek out the Virgin Mary. Niklashausen was only the most dangerous of many such pilgrimage manias. Rather than treat that popular energy with disdain, Bishop Rudolph tried to legitimize it. Knowing there was great popular hunger for the veneration of Mary, he offered forty days' indulgence—the standard amount—to pilgrims who visited the Marian shrines of Scheeberg and Retzbach, two safe, established shrines in the diocese of Würzburg. He did not do so in direct response to the debacle at Niklashausen, but much later, in 1485, as part of his ongoing reform program.

Bishop Rudolph did many other things to reform the church. But did any of it work? Or a better question: How do we measure "success" in church reform? We may look at it negatively, that is, by measuring social unrest quantitatively and then assuming that it is a direct response to the lack of reform. But the assumption is false. Popular movements and uprisings did not necessarily have anything to do with how the official church behaved or did not behave. We cannot understand societies by such simple stimulus-response models. The outburst at Niklashausen, after all, took place during the rule of the best of the reforming bishops, and the populace of the diocese of Würzburg was quiet during the irresponsible, oppressive reigns of Johann von Brun and Johann von Grumbach. Bishop Rudolph's biographer, Siegmund Freiherr von Pölnitz, argues that the bishop's reforms bore fruit as evidenced by the generosity of the wills of laymen toward the church, the poor, and the sick. The argument is specious at best, because we do not have comparative information from Bishop Rudolph's predecessors; and a causal link between generous wills and ecclesiastical reform has not, and perhaps cannot, be made. Generous wills may in fact show the ineffectiveness of the church's attempts to solve real social problems of poverty and the distribution of wealth: people may have taken upon themselves to do what the church could not do.

No, the significance of the reforming zeal of a bishop like Rudolph von Sherenberg seems to be that he pointed out the shortcomings of the clergy for all to see. He justified anticlericalism. He brought before the public eye Christian ideals of poverty, simplicity, and generosity—against which clever laymen such as Hans Behem could measure the lords and the clergy.

Of all the characters in the story, the most elusive is Hans Behem, the Drummer of Niklashausen. We have only sketchy evidence of his rank and status. Even his age is a mystery, although his followers called him "the Youth." We see Hans almost exclusively through the eyes of his enemies—eyes that are never sympathetic, eyes always filled with mocking hatred.

From the very first, Hans was a strange enigma to authorities. Archbishop Dieter wrote Bishop Rudolph on June 13 in our earliest reference to Hans that "lately we learned that a youth [*adolescentem*], a certain Hans Behem, a layman of your diocese, is widely discussed everywhere" as a visionary. Only by the end of June did authorities refer to Hans as "the Drummer." They now knew him to have been a street musician and composer of dangerous pilgrimage songs, which they promptly prohibited people from singing [*das nyemants die liedlin und cantilene von dem peuker gedicht singe*].

The anonymous writer of Eichstätt added two items to our early composite picture of Hans Behem that were probably too obvious for others to mention. Hans, he said, was a *rusticus,* that is, a peasant or a serf, and he was *indoctus,* that is, unlearned or illiterate.

Only gradually did a picture of the strange young man emerge in the minds of authorities. To Bishop Rudolph, the Drummer came to be a *leichtvertigen person,* that is, unscrupulous, perhaps frivolous or thoughtless. That is the phrase he used in his many letters to princes asking for prohibitions of pilgrimages to Niklashausen. He acknowledged Hans' nimble cleverness and suggested that Hans was a cunning rogue who said dangerous things and composed dangerous songs. Bishop Rudolph implied that Hans was driven by evil spirits. This was his assessment after he had met Hans personally, after the interrogation, after Hans' execution. Hans was clearly a clever, dangerous young man, and, so thought the bishop, was responsible for the whole affair.

It is not until 1493, seventeen years after the pilgrimage, that we hear a new interpretation of the Drummer. It appears in a widely distributed, printed edition of Hartmann Schedel's *Liber chronicarum.* Schedel's narrative of the events in Niklashausen is brief and uninteresting. But it is accompanied by a woodcut (see the frontispiece of this book) that shows the Drummer preaching from a window of a cottage to a group of pilgrims sitting on benches who also are listening to another layman. Behind Hans is a man, apparently in a friar's cowl, who seems to be whispering in the Drummer's ear. The artist is arguing that Hans was a mere tool of more crafty men who manipulated him behind the scenes. In other words, the whole affair was a conspiracy, presumably by a lone friar. The artist may have relied for his interpretation on an oral tradition of Hans' "confession" under torture (as reported much later in 1514 by Johann Trithemius). Schedel's printed *Liber chronicarum* directly influenced almost all later accounts of the affair. By 1550 this pictorial interpretation had become hard fact.

About 1500, Konrad Stolle wrote in his *Thüringishe-Erfurtishe Chronik* a long and strangely detailed account of the Drummer and the pilgrimage to Niklashausen. I say strange because there is no precedent for some of his facts; they seem to have been invented for maximum emotional impact. It is Stolle who tells us that the Drummer was arrested at night while preaching naked in a tavern. Naked? Preaching in a tavern in the middle of the night? Surely no earlier writer would have missed this juicy detail. But it suited Stolle's purpose to denigrate the Drummer as much as possible. He also gives us a new interpretation of the Drummer: Hans was too stupid (a "half-wit," or *eyn halber thore*) to be responsible for this affair and was manipulated by three nobles who pushed him to the forefront in order to make money for themselves from pilgrim offerings. In other words, commoners do not make history, even rude and raucous history, nobles do. He identifies them as two "von Stetten" and a priest, "Conrad Thunfeld"! Conrad von Thunfeld, instead of being a knight (as we know he was), has been mistakenly transformed into a priest, apparently the priest of Niklashausen. The three men told Hans what to preach, says Stolle. They told him to fabricate the story of the visions of the Virgin and to call for a pilgrimage to make offerings to her shrine. Thus, within a generation of the pilgrimage, Stolle has given us a full-blown conspiracy theory with strong aristocratic overtones and confused facts.

Johann Trithemius, whom I have often quoted, wrote two accounts of the affair, a short one around 1506, and a longer one in 1514. In his first account, Trithemius says that Hans preached from a window with a certain "fugitive monk" at his side who told him what to say. This is an accurate description of Schedel's woodcut. In the second account in 1514, he elaborates that a certain mendicant friar whispered to the Drummer from his own concealment because the Youth did not speak well and was uneducated. Trithemius also claims that Hans confessed under torture that everything had been fabricated by the "wandering, cunning mendicant friar" and that after the Drummer's arrest the friar fled as far away as possible—and out of our story.

Was there ever such a confession pointing to a concealed monk or friar? Only Trithemius mentions it. Was he relying on court records or on an accepted tradition of a mastermind friar, that is, on a conspiracy theory? We don't know. But we do know that Trithemius was a Benedictine abbot and no friend of the friars. He was also an intellectual who never disguised his contempt for the illiterate, uneducated masses. If Hans was an idiot, a half-wit, and a fool, so his argument goes, then he could not have devised such an astonishing affair alone. There must have been a conspiracy by somebody *educated*. At one point in his account, Trithemius loses patience with the whole affair. He shouts at us about the foolishness of Hans and the stupidity of those who followed him. *Mira stultorum insania,* he cries out—"Look in wonder at the insanity of the stupid people." *Miranda populi furentis etsi stulta confidentia!*—"Marvel at the madness of the people and their stupid confidence!" Novelties. Foolish people will always chase after foolish novelties which can only lead to attacks on the established faith and the established order, and to demands to be free from financial obligations and landlords (such as Trithemius' monastery).

By about 1540, Johannes Herolt is writing in his chronicle that the Drummer had a "monk" behind him who told him what to say. Georg Widman in his chronicle (about 1544) says it was a Franciscan friar. Lorenz Fries, perhaps the most careful of these sixteenth-century writers and historian of the bishops of Würzburg, says it was the parish priest of Niklashausen who whispered to the Drummer.

Monk, friar, priest. Within a generation or two after Niklashausen, Hans Behem had changed from a clever rogue, responsible for the affair, to a simple-minded, helpless boob who was manipulated by renegade clergy. Writers really did not know who manipulated the Drummer, but they were sure that it was somebody familiar with the Scriptures and with preaching, not a half-witted shepherd. Strangely, they all missed the Beghard Brother as a possible culprit. Of course, the mysterious mastermind was never caught, but he and others like him, sixteenth-century writers seemed to imply, might still be on the loose. Such a conspiracy theory satisfied an aristocratic worldview in the sixteenth century, but it is not compelling today. The world of laymen and peasants was much more articulate than their enemies could imagine.

German peasants knew who their oppressors were, even if they did not understand all the causes of their economic oppression and had to use religious language to describe economic misery. Their economic life after 1476 continued to deteriorate, and it was only a matter of time before they again cried out against the clergy and lords. All economic trends rushed against the poor: population increased, especially after the turn of the sixteenth century; land became increasingly scarce; wages fell; rents and food prices rose; and taxes increased dramatically. In Franconia by 1524, about half a peasant's income was taken by taxes, tolls, and duties. By the early sixteenth century, about half the people in south and central Germany were classified as "propertyless." All the gains of the German peasantry of the late Middle Ages had disappeared. We recall Tawney's metaphor of peasants standing in water up to their necks; the water now lapped against their mouths and noses.

In 1525, the peasantry of southern Germany rose in rebellion against their lords and the seignorial order. Some were led by firebrand, renegade priests such as Thomas Müntzer. Manor houses, estates, and churches were put to flame. Even Würzburg—but not the Frauenberg—was briefly occupied by a peasant army. In their Manifesto of Twelve Articles, peasants listed demands against taxes, duties, and servile labor dues—again, as in 1476. Again, peasants demanded that the woods and rivers be made common. Again, peasants took their stand, calling on the support of the supernatural—

this time they made no appeal to the Virgin Mary, but rather to the "Word of God" contained in the Scriptures. At one point they sought the support of Martin Luther, who had also taken his stand on the Scriptures, and sent him a copy of the Twelve Articles. He answered them with a pamphlet, *Against the Robbing and Murdering Hordes of Peasants,* urging lords to kill rebellious peasants as if they were mad dogs. Luther turned his back on the peasants of Germany just as the Virgin Mary had done a half-century earlier. The revolt failed and the peasant fires again were extinguished. Chroniclers tell us that over one hundred thousand peasants were executed in retribution.

There is no direct connection between the events of 1476 in Niklashausen and those of 1525. Nor was Thomas Müntzer responsible for the Peasants' Revolt of 1525 any more than the Drummer "caused" the pilgrimage to Niklashausen. Both tapped into and responded to a deeper level of social discontent of the German peasantry. Both leaders projected peasant religious fantasies onto the stage of history. They tried to express in religious vocabulary their myriad discontents: their social and economic deterioration and the need to find order and comfort in a chaotic, brutal universe.

The story of the Drummer of Niklashausen, the abortive uprising of the poor and uneducated, and its suppression by those in power in the medieval church is a chilling story—especially in the version told by Trithemius that concludes the previous chapter. It seems to reveal the arrogance of the power-elite, as well as the arrogance of those who wrote the history of the uprising to justify the power-elite. Today, our sentiment is for the simple shepherd, Hans Behem. His execution by fire confirms what we seem to know, or remember, in our collective folk memory, about the brutality of medieval bishops and lords.

But does it? Surely real life is more complex when we chase after real human flesh than when we use clichés.

Bishop Rudolph von Sherenberg of Würzburg was the ideal reforming bishop in a reforming century. He worked tenaciously for what even the Drummer would agree was to be a just, Christian society. Like Hans, Bishop Rudolph in his own fashion attempted to eradicate the corrupted ways of the clergy; he tried to curb their greed and arrogance. He also brought peace to the countryside of Würzburg; he tried to protect his peasants from the moneylenders; he tried to simplify clerical dress and behavior to conform with imagined ideals of the early church. He was also responsible for social order and could not tolerate—who could?—social revolution founded on alleged heavenly visions.

And Johann Trithemius, one of the primary historians of the affair, was no darkly hooded, superstitious fiend. He was a superbly educated intellectual in the German Humanist movement of the early sixteenth century. Before coming to Würzburg in 1506, he had for twenty-three years been abbot of the Benedictine monastery of Burs-feld, where he had built up an academic library renowned throughout Europe. We know that he published more than eighty different works of his own: devotional works, histories, and commentaries on the occult, witchcraft, and cryptography. He was a mainstream, Renais-sance, Humanist writer—which is to say, a mouthpiece for the power-elite. Trithemius' contempt for Hans may be paralleled by our own intellectual contempt for TV preachers and leaders of populist religious movements. When was the last time *you* sang in the victory chapel, brother?

No, the Drummer, the bishop, and the historian, all acted out their lives in an illusory, enchanted world in which they saw only darkly the true, divine mainsprings of history. They all would have agreed that the world they experienced was a sort of illusion that veils a greater mystery of the wills and actions of supernatural beings, God, saints, and devils. And they all would have agreed that behind the individual actions of the supernatural beings was God's great plan of history for the salvation and damnation of souls, carried to fruition by chosen humans.

Today, as historians, we would agree that they acted out their lives in an enchanted world in which "reality" was veiled from everyday experience. The world they experienced, indeed, was a sort of illusion to them. But their enchanted world was not metaphysical as they imagined. What they did not see were the great impersonal forces that drove their lives and their history: weather, demography, economic trends, traditions of thought, and other powerful historical patterns that entangled them in historical time.

"People do not understand the history that they are making," is a commonplace among historians, which implies that only in the future will our actions be understood by future historians; only in the future will historians be able to explain what really created our history, because they alone will be in a position to know how our history was resolved—and even then they probably will disagree about how the resolution was effected. As participants in our history, we cannot know its outcome or how it will be explained in the future. The world we experience, therefore, in the great flow of history, is a sort of illusion. We all dance and posture on the stage of our existence; we try to comprehend our lives in terms of old vocabularies, traditional stories (that is, historical narratives), and statistical patterns that usually reaffirm what we already know and tell us little about causation, yet we are unable to fully comprehend the mysterious historical forces that drive our history into the dark unknown. Only future historians can explain us—or misread us. This is to say that we—however attuned to historical time—also must live in an enchanted world.

# BIBLIOGRAPHY

Most of the primary sources for the story of the Drummer of Niklashausen are in print. The most complete collection, with an accompanying narrative, is Klaus Arnold, *Niklashausen 1476* (Baden-Baden: Verlag Valentin Koerner, 1980). But see Nigel Palmer's review of Arnold in *Medium Aevum,* vol. 57, pp. 331–32; Palmer transcribes a poem about Niklashausen, unknown to Arnold, from a Munich manuscript.

An older collection of documents is in K. A. Barack, "Hans Böhm und die Wallfahrt nach Niklashausen im Jahre 1476: ein Vorspiel des großen Bauernkrieges," *Archiv des historischen Vereines von Unterfranken und Aschaffenburg,* 14 (1858), 1–108.

Other source materials are as follows:

# Bibliography

Beyschlag, Fr. "Zur kirchlichen Geschichte der Würzburger Diözese im 15. Jahrhundert," *Beiträge zur bayerischen Kirchengeschichte*, vol. 15, pp. 81–97.

Brant, Sebastian. *The Ship of Fools*. Trans. William Gillis. London: The Folio Society, 1971.

Strauss, Gerald (ed.). *Manifestations of Discontent in Germany on the Eve of the Reformation*. Bloomington: Indiana University Press, 1971.

Thiele, Richard (ed.). "Memoriale—thüringische-erfurtische Chronik—von Konrad Stolle," *Geschichtsquellen der Provinz Sachsen und angrenzender Gebiete*, 39 (1900), 379–83.

Thoma, Albrecht. "Der Pfeifer von Niklashausen: Ein Vorspiel der Reformationszeit," *Preußische Jahrbücher*, 60 (1887), 541–79.

Other primary and secondary materials that I have used are listed below:

Abel, Wilhelm. *Geschichte der deutschen Landwirtschaft vom frühen Mittelalter bis zum 19. Jahrhundert*. Stuttgart: Eugen Ulmer, 1962.

———. *Massenarmut und Hungerkrisen im vorindustriellen Deutschland*. Göttingen: Vanderhoeck and Ruprecht, 1972.

Andreas, Willy. *Deutschland vor der Reformation: Eine Zeitenwende*. Stuttgart: Deutsche Verlags, 1948.

Bakhtin, Mikhail. *Rabelais and His World*. Trans. Hélène Iswolsky. Bloomington: Indiana University Press, 1984.

Barraclough, G. *The Origins of Modern Germany*. New York: Capricorn Books, 1963.

Beissel, Stephan. *Geschichte der Verehrung Marias in Deutschland während des Mittelalters*. Darmstadt: Wissenschaftliche Buchgesellschaft, 1972 [orig. 1909].

Bell, Clair Hayden. *Peasant Life in Old German Epics: 'Meir Helmbrecht' and 'Der Arme Heinrich.'* Trans. C. H. Bell. New York: Columbia University Press, 1931.

Blickle, Peter. "Peasant Revolts in the German Empire in the Late Middle Ages," *Social History*, 4 (1979), 223–39.

———. *The Revolution of 1525: The German Peasants' War from a New Perspective*. Trans. Thomas A. Brady, Jr., and H. C. Erik Midelfort. Baltimore: The Johns Hopkins University Press, 1981.

Bødker, Laurits. *Folk Literature (Germanic)*. Copenhagen: Rosenkilde and Bagger, 1965.

Böhme, Franz M. *Geschichte des Tanzes in Deutschland*. 2 vols. Leipzig: Breitkoff and Härtel, 1886.

Brückner, Wolfgang. "Popular Piety in Central Europe." Trans. Stephen Wedgwood, *Journal of the Folklore Institute*, 5 (1968), 158–74.

——— (ed.). *Volkserzählung und Reformation*. Berlin: Erich Schmidt, 1974.

# Bibliography

Burke, Peter. *Popular Culture in Early Modern Europe.* New York: Harper and Row, 1978.

Chambers, E. K. *The Medieval Stage.* 2 vols. Oxford: Oxford University Press, 1903.

Clemen, Otto. *Die Volksfrömmigkeit des ausgehenden Mittelalters.* Dresden and Leipzig: Ludwig Ungelenk, 1937.

Cohn, Henry J. *The Government of the Rhine Palatinate in the Fifteenth Century.* Oxford: Oxford University Press, 1965.

Cohn, Norman. *The Pursuit of the Millennium.* Revised ed. New York: Oxford University Press, 1970.

Crane, Thomas F. (ed.). *The Exempla or Illustrative Stories from the Sermones Vulgares of Jacques de Vitry.* London: Folk Lore Society, vol. 26, 1890.

Cruel, R. *Geschichte der deutschen Predigt im Mittelalter.* Detmold: Meyerishe Hobbuchhandlung, 1879.

Droege, Georg. "Die finanziellen Grundlagen des Territorialstaates im West- und Ostdeutschland an der Wende vom Mittelalter zur Neuzeit," *Vierteljahrsschrift für Sozial- und Wirtschaftsgeschichte,* 53 (1966), 145–61.

Du Boulay, F. R. H. *Germany in the Later Middle Ages.* New York: St. Martin's Press, 1983.

Franz, Adolph. *Die kirchlichen Benedictionen im Mittelalter.* 2 vols. Graz, Austria: Akademische Druck- u. Verlangsanstalt, 1960.

Franz, Günter. *Geschichte des deutschen Bauernstandes vom frühen Mittelalter bis zum 19. Jahrhundert.* 2d ed. Stuttgart: Eugen Ulmer, 1972.

Frazer, James. *The Golden Bough: A Study in Magic and Religion.* Abridged ed. New York: Macmillan, 1949.

Furnivall, Frederick J. *Bishop Percy's Folio Manuscript: Loose and Humorous Songs.* London: Printed by and for the Editor, 1868.

Haupt, H. "Zur Geschichte der Kinderwallfahrten der Jahre 1455–1459," *Zeitschrift für Kirchengeschichte,* 16 (1896), 672–75.

Heers, Jacques. *Fêtes, Jeux et Joutes dans les sociétés d'occident à la fin du Moyen Age.* Montreal: l'Institut d'études médiévales, 1971.

Hofer, John. *St. John Capistran: Reformer.* Trans. Patrick Cummins. London: B. Herder Book Co., 1943.

Holmes, George. *Europe: Hierarchy and Revolt, 1320–1450.* New York: Harper and Row, 1976.

Kultisher, Josef. *Allgemeine Wirtschaftsgeschichte des Mittelalters und der Neuzeit.* 2 vols. Munich and Vienna: R. Oldenbourg, 1965.

Ladurie, Emmanuel Le Roy. *Carnival in Romans.* Trans. Mary Feeney. New York: George Braziller, Inc., 1979.

———. *Times of Feast, Times of Famine: A History of Climate since the Year 1000.* Trans. Barbara Bray. New York: Doubleday and Co., 1971.

Leach, E. R. *Rethinking Anthropology.* London: Athelone Press, 1961.

Lefebvre, Joël. *Les Fols et la Folie: Etude sur les genres du comique et la création littéraire en Allemagne pendent la Renaissance.* Paris: Libraire C. Klinck-sieck, 1968.
Le Goff, Jacques. *The Birth of Purgatory.* Trans. Arthur Goldhammer. Chicago: University of Chicago Press, 1984.
Lerner, Robert J. "Medieval Prophecy and Religious Dissent," *Past and Present,* 72 (1976), 3–24.
———. *The Heresy of the Free Spirit in the Later Middle Ages.* Berkeley: University of California Press, 1972.
Levack, Brian P. *The Witch-Hunt in Early Modern Europe.* New York: Long-man, Inc., 1987.
Lévy-Bruhl, Lucien. *How Natives Think.* Trans. Lilian A. Clare. London: George Allen and Unwin Ltd., 1926.
Lewis, I. M. *Social Anthropology in Perspective: The Relevance of Social Anthropology.* Harmondsworth: Penguin, 1976.
Lewis, Oscar. *Anthropological Essays.* New York: Random House, 1970.
Little, A. G. (ed.). *Liber Exemplorum ad usum Praedicantium: Saeculo XIII compositus a quodam fratre minore anglico de provincia Hiberniae.* Aber-doniae: Typis Academicis, 1908.
Little, Lester K. *Religious Poverty and the Profit Economy in Medieval Europe.* Ithaca: Cornell University Press, 1978.
McGinn, Bernard. *Visions of the End: Apocalyptic Traditions in the Middle Ages.* New York: Columbia University Press, 1979.
Miskimin, Harry A. *The Economy of Early Renaissance Europe, 1300–1460.* Englewood Cliffs: Prentice Hall, 1969.
———. *The Economy of Later Renaissance Europe, 1460–1600.* Cambridge: Cambridge University Press, 1977.
Mols, Roger. *Introduction à la démographie historique des villes d'Europe du XIV⁰ au XVIII⁰ siècle.* 3 vols. Louvain: Bibliothèque de l'université, 1954–1956.
Neumann, Erich. *The Great Mother: An Analysis of the Archetype.* Trans. Ralph Manheim. 2d ed. Princeton: Princeton University Press, 1963.
Owst, G. R. *Preaching in Medieval England.* New York: Russell and Russell, Inc., 1965 [orig. 1926].
Ozment, Steven (ed.). *The Reformation in Medieval Perspective.* Chicago: Quadrangle Books, 1971.
Peters, Edward. *Torture.* Oxford: Basil Blackwell, 1985.
———. *The Magician, the Witch, and the Law.* Philadelphia: University of Pennsylvania Press, 1978.
Peuckert, Will-Erich. *Die Grosse Wende: Das apokalyptische Saeculum und Luther.* Hamburg: Claassen and Goverts, 1948.
Pfander, Homer G. *The Popular Sermon of the Medieval Friar in England.* New York: New York University, 1937.
Pfannmüller, D. G., and Berger, Arnold E. *Lied-, Spruch-, und Fabeldichtung in Dienste der Reformation.* Leipzig: Philipp Reclam, Jr., 1938.

# Bibliography

Redfield, Robert. *Peasant Society and Culture: An Anthropological Approach to Civilization*. Chicago: University of Chicago Press, 1956.
————. *The Little Community: Viewpoints for the Study of a Human Whole*. Chicago: University of Chicago Press, 1955.
Reeves, Marjorie. "Some Popular Prophecies from the Fourteenth to the Seventeenth Centuries," *Studies in Church History*, 8 (1971), 107–34.
————. *The Influence of Prophecy in the Later Middle Ages: A Study of Joachism*. Oxford: Clarendon Press, 1969.
Rich, E. E., and Wilson, C. H. (eds.). *The Cambridge Economic History of Europe. Vol IV: The Economy of Expanding Europe in the Sixteenth and Seventeenth Centuries*. Cambridge: Cambridge University Press, 1967.
Rudwin, Maximilian. *The Origin of the German Carnival Comedy*. New York: G. E. Stechert and Co., 1920.
Russell, J. C. "Late Mediaeval Population Patterns," *Speculum*, 20 (1945), 157–71.
Sabean, David. "The Communal Basis of Pre-1800 Peasant Uprisings in Western Europe," *Comparative Politics*, 3 (1976), 355–64.
Schreiber, Georg, et al. *Wallfahrt und Volkstum in Geschichte und Leben*. Düsseldorf: L. Schwann, 1934.
Scribner, Bob, and Benecke, Gerhard (eds.). *The German Peasant War of 1525—New Viewpoints*. London: George Allen and Unwin, 1979.
Scribner, R. W. *Popular Culture and Popular Movements in Reformation Germany*. London: Hambledon Press, 1987.
Sharbrough, Steven. "El Ciclo de los Pastores," *History of Religions at UCLA Newsletter*, 3 (1975), 7–11.
Southern, R. W. *Western Society and the Church in the Middle Ages*. Harmondsworth: Penguin, 1970.
Stover, Leon. *The Cultural Ecology of Chinese Civilization: Peasants and Elites in the Last of the Agrarian States*. New York: Pica Press, 1974.
Strauss, Gerald. *Pre-Reformation Germany*. London: Macmillan, 1972.
Stuart, H. S. M. (ed.). *The Autobiography of Götz von Berlichingen*. London: Gerald Duckworth and Co. 1956.
Sumberg, Samuel L. *The Nuremberg Shembart Carnival*. New York: AMS Press, 1966 [orig. 1941].
Sumption, Jonathan. *Pilgrimage: An Image of Medieval Religion*. London: Faber and Faber, 1975.
Tawney, R. L. *Land and Labour in China*. London: George Allen and Unwin Ltd., 1932.
Thompson, W. D. J. Cargill. "Seeing the Reformation in Medieval Perspective," *Journal of Ecclesiastical History*, 25 (1974), 297–308.
Thrupp, Sylvia (ed.). *Change in Medieval Society: Europe North of the Alps, 1050–1500*. New York: Appleton-Century-Crofts, 1964.

# Bibliography

————. *Millennial Dreams in Action: Essays in Comparative Studies.* The Hague: Mouton and Co., 1962.

Trüdinger, Karl. *Stadt und Kirche im spätmittelalterlichen Würzburg.* Stuttgart: Klett-Cotta, 1978.

Turner, Victor, and Turner, Edith. *Image and Pilgrimage in Christian Culture: Anthropological Perspectives.* Oxford: Basil Blackwell, 1978.

Villari, P. *Life and Times of Girolamo Savonarola.* London: T. Fisher Unwin, 1896.

von Below, Georg. *Territorium und Stadt.* 2d ed. Munich and Berlin: R. Oldenbourg, 1923.

von Pölnitz, Sigmund Freiherr. "Die bischöfliche Reformarbeit im Hochstift Würzburg während des 15. Jahrhunderts: Unter besonderer Berücksichtigung der übrigen fränkischen Diözesen," *Würzburger Diözenangeschichtsblätter,* 8/9 (1940–41), 4–168.

Vovelle, Gaby and Michel. *Vision de la mort et de l'au-delà en Provence: d'auprès les autels des âmes du purgatoire XVe–XXe siècles. Cahiers des Annals,* 29. Paris, 1970.

Vovelle, Michel. *La mort et l'occident de 1300 à nos jours.* Paris: Gallimard, 1983.

Warner, Marina. *Alone of All Her Sex: The Myth and the Cult of the Virgin Mary.* New York: Alfred A. Knopf, 1976.

Wattenbach, W. "Beiträge zur Geschichte der Mark Brandenburg aus Handschriften der königlichen Bibliothek," *Akademie der Wissenschaften,* (1882), 587–609.

Welter, J.-Th. *Littérature religieuse et didactique du Moyen Age.* Paris: Occitania, 1927.

Whitrow, G. W. *Time in History: The Evolution of Our General Awareness of Time and Temporal Perspective.* Oxford: Oxford University Press, 1988.

Wolf, Eric R. *Peasants.* Englewood Cliffs: Prentice Hall, 1966.

Young, Karl. *The Drama of the Medieval Church.* 2 vols. Oxford: Clarendon Press, 1933.

Zawart, Anscar. *The History of Franciscan Preaching and Franciscan Preachers (1209–1927): A Bio-Bibliographical Study.* New York: Franciscan Studies No. 7, 1928.

Zika, Charles. "Hosts, Processions and Pilgrimages: Controlling the Sacred in Fifteenth-Century Germany," *Past and Present,* 118 (1988), 25–64.

RICHARD WUNDERLI is Professor of
History at the University of Colorado,
Colorado Springs, and author of *London
Church Courts and Society on the Eve of the
Reformation.*